PRENTICE HALL **Science**
Explorer

Standardized Test Preparation Workbook

PEARSON
Prentice
Hall

Boston, Massachusetts
Upper Saddle River, New Jersey

Pearson Prentice Hall™ is a trademark of Pearson Education, Inc.
Pearson® is a registered trademark of Pearson plc.
Prentice Hall® is a registered trademark of Pearson Education, Inc.

ISBN 0-13-125633-5

6 7 8 9 10   10 09 08 07 06

TABLE OF CONTENTS

These *SAT9, ITBS, TerraNova Practice Tests* and *National Assessment of Educational Progress* have been created based on content objectives and in formats similar to actual tests. See *Progress Monitoring Assessments* book for answers to all Practice Tests.

Grade 6 Practice Tests

Grade 7 Practice Tests

Grade 8 Practice Tests

SAT9 PREP   **GRADE 6 PRACTICE TEST**

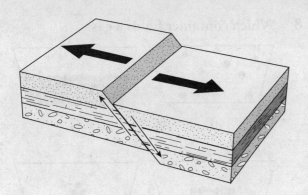

1 The diagram shows a fault caused by tension forces. **What type of fault is it?**

   A Strike-slip fault
   B Normal fault
   C Abnormal fault
   D Reverse fault

2 **Which of these organisms is a protist?**

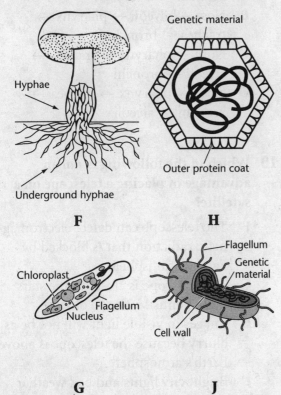

3 In a lab burner, methane reacts with oxygen to produce carbon dioxide and water: $CH_4 + 2O_2 \rightarrow CO_2 + 2H_2O$. **What are the reactants in this reaction?**

   A $CH_4 + CO_2$
   B $O_2 + H_2O$
   C $CO_2 + H_2O$
   D $CH_4 + O_2$

Directions: Use the information below to answer questions 4–5.

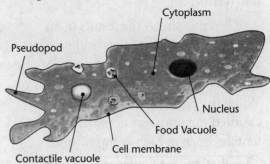

4 **How does the food vacuole form?**

   F It forms through binary fission.
   G It forms when the cell membrane divides.
   H It forms when cytoplasm flows away from food particles.
   J It forms when the ends of two pseudopods join together.

5 An amoeba is a unicellular organism that lacks a cell wall. It can move from place to place to obtain food by eating other organisms. **Scientists classify amoebas as —**

   A animals
   B bacteria
   C fungi
   D protists

GO ON

SAT9 PREP GRADE 6 PRACTICE TEST *(continued)*

6 Which divisions of time are the longest?

F Eras   **H** Epochs
G Periods   **J** Centuries

Directions: Use the information and the table below to answer question 7.

Alligators are large reptiles with muscular tails, large teeth, and strong jaws. Like nearly all reptiles, alligators hatch from eggs.

The table shows the results of an experiment conducted with alligator eggs. Scientists incubated the eggs of one alligator species at different temperatures. When the eggs hatched, the scientists counted the numbers of males and females born in each group of eggs.

Incubation Temperature	Number of Females	Number of Males
29.4°C	80	0
30.6°C	19	13
31.7°C	13	38
32.8°C	0	106

7 What question were the scientists most likely trying to answer?

A Does the body temperature of newborn alligators depend on the incubation temperature?

B Do different alligator species hatch at different incubation temperatures?

C Do high incubation temperatures prevent alligator eggs from hatching?

D Does the incubation temperature of the eggs affect the sex of the alligators?

8 Which container holds a gas?

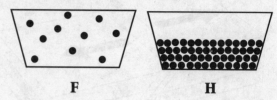

F   H

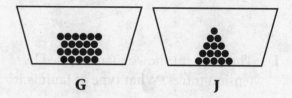

G   J

9 Which of the following shows the correct path of air through the human respiratory system?

A Nose → trachea → esophagus → bronchi → alveoli

B Nose → alveoli → pharynx → trachea → bronchi

C Nose → pharynx → trachea → alveoli → bronchi

D Nose → pharynx → trachea → bronchi → alveoli

10 Which of the following is *not* an advantage of placing a telescope on a satellite?

F The telescope can detect electromagnetic radiation that is blocked by Earth's atmosphere.

G The telescope is closer to the stars that scientists want to observe.

H Images in visible light will not be as blurry because the telescope is above Earth's atmosphere.

J Bright city lights and bad weather will not interfere with observations.

SAT9 PREP GRADE 6 PRACTICE TEST *(continued)*

11 Which graph represents the growth of the human population in the last 3,000 years?

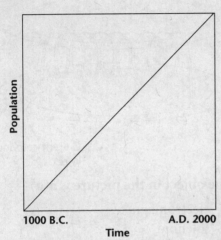

A

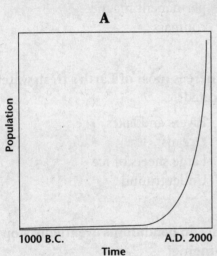

B

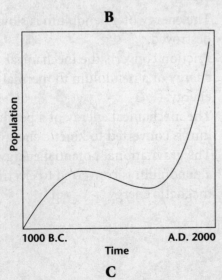

C

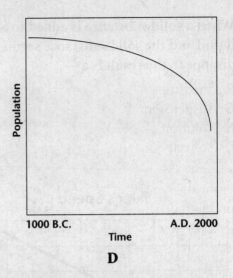

D

12 What does the color of a star indicate?

   F Its density

   G Its temperature

   H Its distance from Earth

   J Its brightness

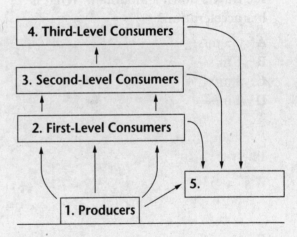

13 In this food web, the number five level includes bacteria and fungi. **What are the organisms in the number five level called?**

   A Herbivores

   B Decomposers

   C Scavengers

   D Carnivores

GO ON

14 When a solid substance is added to a liquid and the solid substance seems to disappear, the result is a —

F   mixture
G   suspension
H   solution
J   solvent

Skier's Speed

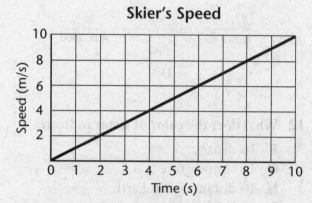

15 The graph above shows a skier's speed as she travels down a mountain. **What is her acceleration?**

A   0.5 m/s^2
B   1 m/s^2
C   2 m/s^2
D   4 m/s^2

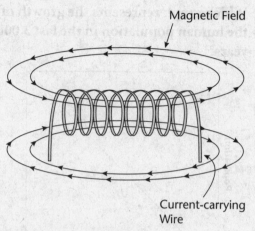

Magnetic Field

Current-carrying Wire

16 The object in the picture is a(n) —

F   electromagnet
G   solenoid
H   permanent magnet
J   compass

17 Where is most of Earth's fresh water located?

A   Rivers and lakes
B   Oceans
C   Large sheets of ice
D   Underground

18 Why do pendulums eventually stop swinging?

F   The energy of a pendulum is slowly destroyed.
G   Friction converts the mechanical energy of a pendulum to thermal energy.
H   The mechanical energy of a pendulum is converted to kinetic energy.
J   The gravitational potential energy of a pendulum is converted to electromagnetic energy.

GO ON

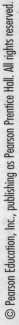

19 A human body cell has 46 chromosomes. How many chromosomes will each of its daughter cells have?

A 23 (46 ÷ 2)   C 92 (46 × 2)

B 46   D 184 (46 × 4)

Directions: Use the information and the table below to answer question 20.

A researcher wondered how salinity affects the speed of sound in water. Salinity is a measure of the concentration of dissolved salt in water. The researcher used a sonar device to measure the depth of both a freshwater lake and a saltwater lake. She also measured the time it took for the sound waves produced by the sonar device to travel from the surface to the bottom of each lake and back again. The average temperature of the water in both lakes was 20 degrees Celsius. The researcher's data are shown in the table below.

Type of Lake	Depth (m)	Time for Sound Waves to Travel from Surface to Bottom and Back to Surface (s)
Freshwater	54.1	0.0730
Saltwater	12.0	0.0158

20 Based on the data in the table, how does salinity affect the speed of sound in water?

F Salinity has no effect on the speed of sound in water.

G The speed of sound in water increases with increasing salinity.

H The speed of sound in water decreases with increasing salinity.

J Sound waves cannot travel through water with high salinity.

21 Which of the following organisms is an angiosperm?

A Moss   C Yeast

B Dandelion   D Fern

22 What is the energy source that drives the processes in the water cycle?

F Heat energy from deep within Earth

G The sun's energy

H Static electricity from lightning

J Energy released and absorbed when water changes state

23 Which of the following is *not* an example of homeostasis?

A As a person's body temperature rises, the person begins to sweat.

B As a person's muscle cells use more oxygen, the person's breathing rate decreases.

C As a person's skin cells are shed, more skin cells are produced.

D As a person's body loses water, the person becomes thirsty.

24 What device changes the voltage from 2,400 V to 120 V before electricity enters a house?

F Commutator   H Transformer

G Galvanometer   J Electric meter

GO ON

25 Which of these organisms stays in one place like a plant, but is an animal because it takes in food?

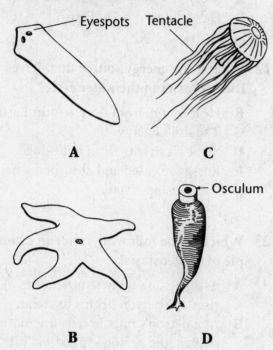

26 Why do climates near the equator tend to be warmer than other areas on Earth?

F These regions receive less direct sunlight.

G These regions receive more direct sunlight.

H These regions are closer to the sun.

J These regions have fewer clouds to block the sunlight.

27 Both of the hydrocarbons below have the same molecular formula, C_4H_{10}, but their atoms are arranged differently. **What are these two molecules?**

A Isomers   **C** Polymers

B Isotopes   **D** Allotropes

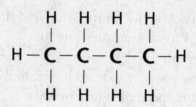

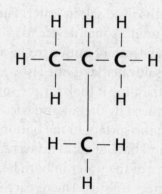

28 Which of the following is *not* an organ of excretion?

F The kidneys

G The skin

H The lungs

J The pancreas

29 Most volcanoes are found —

A near plate boundaries

B along the rim of the Atlantic Ocean

C in the interior of large continental plates

D above hot spots in the mantle

GO ON

SAT9 PREP GRADE 6 PRACTICE TEST *(continued)*

30 The troposphere gets most of its heat through the process shown in the diagram. **What type of heat transfer is represented?**

F Reflection
G Radiation
H Conduction
J Convection

31 When a tornado has been seen in the sky or on weather radar in your area, the National Weather Service issues a —

A tornado warning
B tornado alert
C tornado watch
D tornado hazard

32 In the periodic table, elements with similar properties are found in the same —

F group   H row
G period   J series

33 What type of front forms when cold air moves underneath warm air, forcing the warm air to rise?

A A warm front
B A cold front
C A stationary front
D An occluded front

Directions: Use the illustration below to answer questions 34–35.

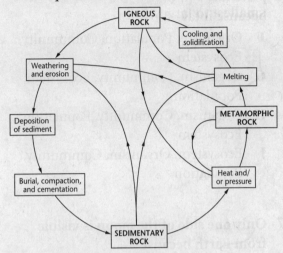

34 **What is the first process that occurs during the formation of sedimentary rock?**

F Existing rock is weathered and eroded.
G Sediment is buried and compacted.
H Existing rock is melted.
J Buried sediment is cemented together.

35 **What process must occur for igneous rock to form from existing rock?**

A Heat must melt the rock.
B The rock must be eroded.
C Pressure must act on the rock.
D Lava must erupt from a volcano.

GO ON

SAT9 PREP GRADE 6 PRACTICE TEST *(continued)*

36 Which of the following lists shows the levels of ecological organization from smallest to largest?

F Organism, Population, Community, Ecosystem

G Organism, Community, Ecosystem, Population

H Organism, Community, Population, Ecosystem

J Ecosystem, Organism, Community, Population

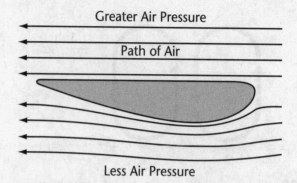

Greater Air Pressure

Path of Air

Less Air Pressure

37 Only one side of the moon is visible from Earth because —

A the moon does not rotate on its axis

B the moon does not revolve around Earth

C the moon is in a geosynchronous orbit around Earth

D the moon revolves once and rotates once in the same period of time

40 The shape of this object causes air to move faster below it than above it. **What is this object?**

F An airplane wing, because air pressure pushes it upward, creating lift

G A spoiler on a racing car, because air pressure pushes it downward, creating better traction

H A bird wing, because air pressure pushes it downward, creating lift

J A sail on a ship, because air pressure pushes it forward, creating a buoyant force

38 Which of the following involves a chemical change?

F Water freezes to become ice.

G Two substances combine to form a third substance.

H Dry ice sublimes to become carbon dioxide gas.

J Glass breaks into small pieces.

39 Which of these actions is a voluntary response?

A Sneezing

B Breathing

C Chewing

D An increase in heartbeat rate

ITBS PREP　　　　　　　　　　　　　　　**GRADE 6 PRACTICE TEST**

1 In an experiment studying the effects of acid rain on pond water, which of the following could be the control?

　A A container of vinegar to represent the acid
　B The pond
　C A container of pond water with nothing added to it
　D A container of pond water with acid added to it

2 A change in an organism's surroundings that causes it to react is called —

　J a response
　K a stimulus
　L energy
　M development

3 The two most abundant gases in the atmosphere are —

　A carbon dioxide and oxygen
　B carbon dioxide and nitrogen
　C nitrogen and oxygen
　D nitrogen and hydrogen

4 When you turn on a toaster, stove, or microwave oven, you are converting electrical energy into —

　J thermal energy
　K mechanical energy
　L nuclear energy
　M magnetic energy

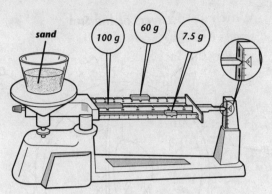

5 A container of sand is weighed using a triple-beam balance, as shown above. If the mass of the container is 14.5 grams, what is the mass of the sand?

　A 93 g
　B 145.5 g
　C 153 g
　D 167.5 g

6 Which of the following characteristics do all plants share?

　J Being unicellular
　K Producing flowers
　L Being a prokaryote
　M Being an autotroph

GO ON

Layers of the Sun

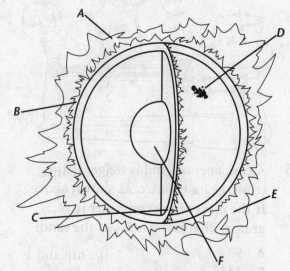

7 Which letter or letters identify the chromosphere in this diagram of the structures of the sun?

A A and E   C C and D
B B   D F

8 The tendency of an object to resist change in its motion is known as —

J mass   L force
K inertia   M balance

9 What is a hypothesis?

A Any factor that can change in an experiment
B Patterns or trends in the data
C A statement that sums up what you have learned from an experiment
D A possible explanation that is tested by an experiment

10 A diagram that shows the amount of energy that moves from one feeding level to another in a food web is called a(n) —

J food chain
K energy pyramid
L ecosystem
M niche

11 When many layers of thin, runny lava build up a high, level area, the result is a —

A lava plateau
B shield volcano
C cinder cone volcano
D composite volcano

Three States of a Substance

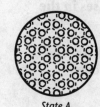

State A   State B   State C

12 Which of the three states represent(s) a solid?

J State A
K State B
L State C
M States B and C

GO ON

ITBS PREP GRADE 6 PRACTICE TEST *(continued)*

13 Which of the following is an advantage of solar energy?

A It will not run out for billions of years.
B It is not available at night.
C No backup energy sources are needed.
D It must be collected from a huge area.

14 Which of the following is a characteristic shared by all animals?

J Their bodies have many cells.
K They eat autotrophs.
L They reproduce asexually.
M They have skeletons.

15 In a circle graph, how many degrees would be in a wedge that represented 50% of the total circle?

A 360°
B 180°
C 90°
D 45°

16 Population density is defined as —

J an approximation of a number, based on reasonable assumptions
K the number of individuals of a population in a specific area
L the number of individuals moving into a population
M the smallest level of ecological organization

After Rubbing

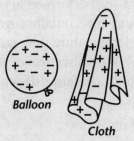

Balloon
Cloth

17 What type of overall charge, if any, does the balloon have after being rubbed with the cloth?

A No overall charge
B A negative charge on the top and a positive charge on the bottom
C A positive charge
D A negative charge

18 The process of change that occurs during an organism's life to produce a more complex organism is called —

J reproduction
K growth
L development
M stimulus

19 In which "sphere" are rivers included?

A Hydrosphere
B Atmosphere
C Biosphere
D Lithosphere

GO ON

20 Natasha is writing a lab report for an experiment she performed in class. She writes, "Water that contains sugar freezes at a lower temperature than water without sugar." **Which section of the lab report should contain this sentence?**

J Hypothesis
K List of materials
L Conclusion
M Observations

21 **The theory that astronomers have developed to describe the formation of the universe is called the —**

A expanding cloud theory
B time warp theory
C galactic expansion theory
D big bang theory

A Plant Cell

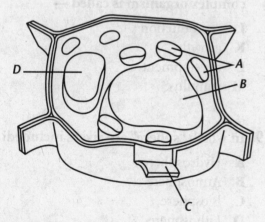

22 **Which structure shown in the diagram is made of cellulose?**

J A   **L** C
K B   **M** D

23 Magnetic poles that are alike —

A attract each other
B repel each other
C do not react to each other
D always point toward the north

24 **Which term refers to the process by which individuals that are better adapted to their environment are more likely to survive and reproduce?**

J Natural selection
K Overproduction
L Competition
M Variation

25 **A graph in which data about separate but related items are represented by rectangular shapes is called a —**

A bar graph
B line graph
C circle graph
D data table

26 **Perspiration helps maintain body temperature by —**

J washing bacteria off the skin
K evaporating and carrying body heat away
L evaporating and saving body heat
M preventing heat from entering the body

GO ON

ITBS PREP GRADE 6 PRACTICE TEST (continued)

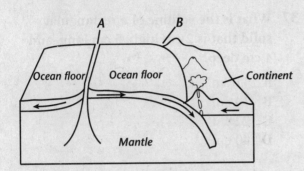

27 What type of boundary is shown at A?

A Mountain range
B Rift valley
C Mid-ocean ridge
D Deep-sea trench

28 Fossil fuels are energy-rich because they contain —

J fossil fragments
K heat
L electricity
M hydrocarbons

29 Factors that control traits are called —

A genes
B purebreds
C recessives
D parents

30 Pure substances formed from chemical combinations of two or more different elements are called —

J elements
K compounds
L mixtures
M solutions

31 An animal has bilateral symmetry if —

A no lines can be drawn to divide the animal into halves that are mirror images
B many lines can be drawn to divide the animal into halves that are mirror images
C one line can be drawn to divide the animal into halves that are mirror images
D any line through the center of the animal divides it into halves that are mirror images

32 The region around a magnet where the magnetic force is exerted is known as its —

J magnetic pole
K lodestone
L magnetic field
M magnetic domain

33 What did Darwin observe about finches in the Galápagos Islands?

A Their feathers were adapted to match their environment.
B Their beaks were adapted to match the foods they ate.
C They had identical phenotypes in all locations.
D They had identical genotypes in all locations.

GO ON

ITBS PREP GRADE 6 PRACTICE TEST *(continued)*

34 **Which of the following statements is an observation about this scene?**

  J The house collapsed at the same time that the poles fell down.

  K The road damage is serious, and it will be very expensive to repair.

  L The house is built on unstable land.

  M The ground is broken.

35 **Air in the atmosphere has pressure because —**

  A the stratosphere is thick

  B air has mass

  C wind moves the air

  D temperature warms the air

36 **The law of conservation of energy states that when one form of energy is converted into another —**

  J energy is destroyed in the process

  K no energy is destroyed in the process

  L energy is created in the process

  M some amount of energy cannot be accounted for

37 **What is the volume of a rectangular solid that is 2 cm high, 5 cm long, and 4 cm deep?**

  A 11 cm³

  B 14 cm³

  C 22 cm³

  D 40 cm³

38 **When you rub your hands together on a cold day, you use friction to convert —**

  J mechanical energy into thermal energy

  K thermal energy into nuclear energy

  L nuclear energy into electrical energy

  M electrical energy into electro-magnetic energy

Pedigree

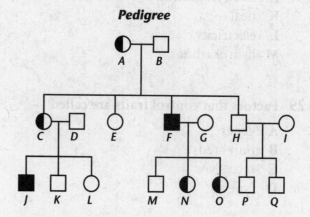

39 **Which individuals have the trait that is traced by the pedigree?**

  A A, C, N, O

  B A, C, F, J, N, O

  C E, G, I, L

  D F, J

GO ON

ITBS PREP GRADE 6 PRACTICE TEST *(continued)*

40 The force that pulls falling objects toward Earth is called —

  J gravity
  K free fall
  L acceleration
  M air resistance

41 The process by which natural forces move weathered rock and soil from one place to another is called —

  A soil conservation
  B deposition
  C abrasion
  D erosion

42 The process by which an organism's internal environment is kept stable in spite of changes in the external environment is called —

  J healing
  K digestion
  L homeostasis
  M respiration

STOP

TERRANOVA PREP **GRADE 6 PRACTICE TEST**

1 One example of changing a substance physically is —

A burning paper
B baking cookies
C heating table sugar
D blending a milkshake

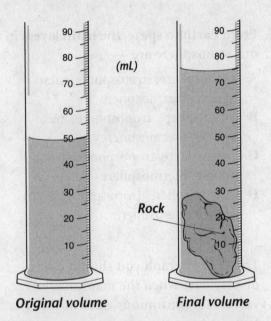

(mL)

Rock

Original volume   Final volume

2 Suppose you need to measure the volume of a rock. You decide to use water and a graduated cylinder to find that measurement. You obtain the results shown above. **What is the volume of the rock?**

F 50 mL
G 75 mL
H 30 mL
J 25 mL

3 What is the correct order of Earth's layers, starting from the surface?

A Crust, outer core, inner core, mantle
B Mantle, outer core, inner core, crust
C Crust, mantle, outer core, inner core
D Outer core, inner core, crust, mantle

4 An organism's scientific name consists of —

F its class name and its family name
G its kingdom name and its phylum name
H its genus name and its species name
J its phylum name and its species name

5 As part of the rock cycle, sedimentary rock attached to an oceanic plate would eventually —

A get thicker and thicker until it rose above sea level
B come to the end of its pathway through the rock cycle
C change to organic rock
D undergo subduction, melt, and form magma

6 Which of the following do all living things need to survive?

F Water
G Oxygen
H Sunlight
J Carbon dioxide

GO ON

7 The heliocentric system gained support when Galileo observed that —

A one side of the moon always faces Earth

B most of the smaller planets are closer to the sun

C Venus goes through phases similar to those of Earth's moon

D the orbit of each planet is an ellipse

8 Which of the following is an example of a scientific question?

F Is experimenting on white mice right or wrong?

G Should scientists make as much money as athletes?

H Does tanning harm the skin?

J Who is the most famous scientist in the world?

Substance	Melting Point (°C)	Boiling Point (°C)
Butane	−138	0
Methanol	−98	65
Heptane	−91	98
Iodine	114	184

9 Which substance is in a liquid state at 150°C?

A Butane

B Heptane

C Iodine

D Methanol

10 Which kingdom includes only prokaryotes?

F Archaebacteria

G Protists

H Plants

J Fungi

11 From Earth to space, the main layers in our atmosphere are —

A troposphere, stratosphere, mesosphere, thermosphere

B stratosphere, troposphere, mesosphere, thermosphere

C mesosphere, troposphere, stratosphere, thermosphere

D thermosphere, troposphere, stratosphere, mesosphere

12 The type of graph you should use to display data when the manipulated variable is continuous, such as time, temperature, or mass, is a —

F bar graph

G line graph

H circle graph

J data table

13 According to Dalton's theory of atoms, all atoms in any element —

A are exactly alike

B can be broken into smaller pieces

C are different

D have a different mass

GO ON

Passive Transport in Red Blood Cells

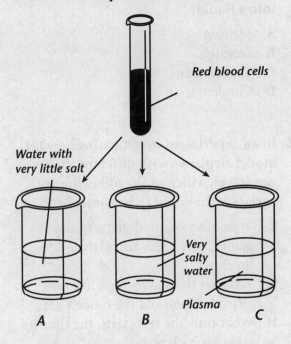

Directions: Use the student notes given below to answer question 16.

I investigated yeast, tiny organisms that give off carbon dioxide gas as they grow. In two bottles, I put 2 mL of yeast, 5 mL of sugar, and water. In Bottle A, I used 250 mL of cold water (20°C). In Bottle B, I used 250 mL of warm water (40°C). I attached a balloon to each bottle. After five minutes, I observed bubbles forming on the surface inside both bottles, and the balloons on both bottles expanded. The balloon on Bottle B became about twice as large as the balloon on Bottle A.

14 Placing red blood cells into which beaker would cause them to shrink?

    F A
    G B
    H C
    J A, B, or C

15 Wetlands help control flooding by —

    A absorbing runoff from heavy rains
    B collecting water behind dams
    C providing natural water filtration
    D quickly releasing water

16 Which statement represents the procedure as it might be written in a lab report based on these notes?

    F Yeast, sugar, warm and cool water, containers, timer
    G Combine the yeast, sugar and water in a bottle. Put a balloon on the bottle.
    H Yeast give off more gas at higher temperatures.
    J If you increase the water temperature, then the yeast will give off more gas.

17 What is the term for an animal that hunts and kills other animals for food?

    A Vertebrate
    B Carnivore
    C Predator
    D Herbivore

TERRANOVA PREP GRADE 6 PRACTICE TEST *(continued)*

18 A solid is a state of matter that has a(n) —

F indefinite volume and an indefinite shape

G definite volume and a definite shape

H definite volume and an indefinite shape

J indefinite volume and a definite shape

North American Air Masses

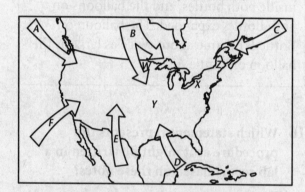

19 Which air masses shown are likely to bring dry weather to the United States?

A A and F

B B and E

C C and D

D D and A

20 How many kilometers are there in 4,500 meters?

F 4,500

G 450

H 45

J 4.5

21 Which process involves a gas changing into a liquid?

A Melting

B Freezing

C Vaporization

D Condensation

22 In an experiment investigating how far model airplanes with different shapes can travel, which of the following are variables that need to be controlled?

F Type of wood used; mass of the planes; glue used; air currents and breezes

G Whether the shapes look like real airplanes; how old the models are

H What time the test starts; the time it takes for each test

J Whether the models land smoothly or become damaged during the test

23 When the temperature of a gas decreases, its —

A pressure increases

B volume increases

C pressure decreases

D particles move faster

24 The large muscle that enables mammals to breathe in and out is called the —

F lung

G respiratory muscle

H cardiac muscle

J diaphragm

GO ON

25 Which of these diagrams of rock stress represents shearing?

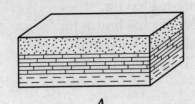

A

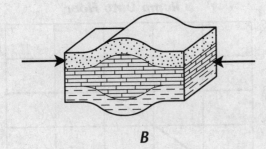

B

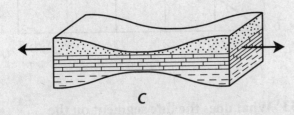

C

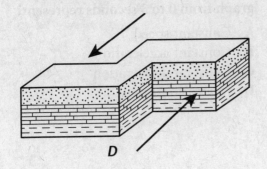

D

Directions: Use the graph below to answer questions 26–27.

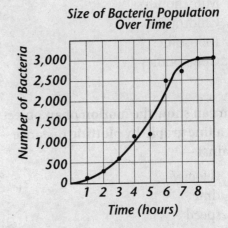

Size of Bacteria Population Over Time

26 What conclusion can you draw from this graph?

F The size of the bacteria population increased steadily until it reached a certain size.

G Bacteria grow faster in sugar water than in plain water.

H After the size of the bacteria population becomes constant, it will decrease rapidly.

J Bacteria can cause disease.

27 How long did it take the bacteria population to reach a constant?

A 2 hours
B 4 hours
C 6 hours
D 8 hours

GO ON

28 Which organelles produce most of a cell's energy?

   F Mitochondria
   G Chloroplasts
   H Ribosomes
   J Golgi bodies

29 You can show the motion of an object on a line graph by plotting distance against —

   A velocity
   B time
   C speed
   D direction

30 Mitosis is the stage during which —

   F the cell's nucleus divides into two new nuclei
   G the cell's DNA is replicated
   H the cell divides into two new cells
   J the cell's cytoplasm divides

31 When an air mass rises up a mountainside —

   A the temperature increases and the relative humidity decreases
   B the temperature increases and the relative humidity increases
   C the temperature decreases and the relative humidity increases
   D the temperature decreases and the relative humidity decreases

32 Which of the following is a quantitative observation?

   F This dog has fur.
   G This dog has brown fur.
   H This dog's fur is shiny.
   J This dog's fur is 5 cm long.

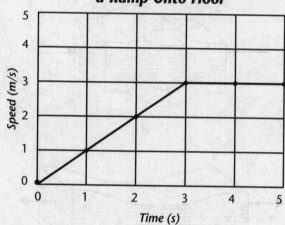

Speed of Ball Rolling Down a Ramp Onto Floor

33 What does the line segment on the graph from 0 to 3 seconds represent?

   A Constant speed
   B Constant acceleration
   C Constant deceleration
   D Decreasing speed

GO ON

TERRANOVA PREP GRADE 6 PRACTICE TEST *(continued)*

34 The many overlapping food chains in an ecosystem make up a(n) —

- **F** food web
- **G** niche
- **H** energy pyramid
- **J** feeding level

35 Geosynchronous satellites above the equator —

- **A** revolve around Earth faster than other satellites
- **B** vary considerably in their distance from Earth
- **C** stay above the same point on Earth
- **D** follow an elliptical orbit

36 Which of the following statements is an inference?

- **F** I hear a dog barking.
- **G** In two weeks, there will be snow on the ground.
- **H** The temperature today is 4°C.
- **J** I smell smoke coming from the pile of wood.

37 Changing direction is an example of a kind of —

- **A** acceleration
- **B** speed
- **C** velocity
- **D** constant rate

U.S. Electricity Production by Energy Source

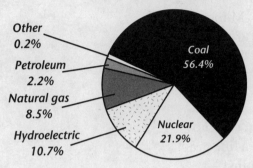

38 Which energy source produces the greatest percentage of electricity?

- **F** Natural gas
- **G** Hydroelectric
- **H** Nuclear
- **J** Coal

39 The measurement of how much matter an object contains is its —

- **A** volume
- **B** weight
- **C** mass
- **D** melting point

40 Solar prominences —

- **F** are cooler than the rest of the chromosphere
- **G** link different parts of sunspot regions together
- **H** cannot be seen during an eclipse
- **J** are hotter than the rest of the chromosphere

STOP

1 Identify the downward fold shown in the rock below.

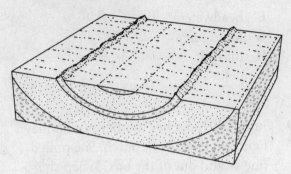

  A   Reverse fault
  B   Syncline
  C   Plateau
  D   Anticline

2 If two compounds in a solution react to form a salt, the reactants were probably —

  F   an acid and a base
  G   a polar molecule and a nonpolar molecule
  H   covalent compounds
  J   a solute and a solvent

3 The sugar glucose ($C_6H_{12}O_6$) is the major source of energy for your body's cells. **Which equation best describes the process of respiration?**

  A $C_6H_{12}O_6 + H_2O + energy \rightarrow CO_2 + O_2$
  B $CO_2 + H_2O + energy \rightarrow C_6H_{12}O_6 + O_2$
  C $C_6H_{12}O_6 + O_2 \rightarrow CO_2 + H_2O + energy$
  D $CO_2 + H_2O \rightarrow C_6H_{12}O_6 + O_2 + energy$

Earth   Star A   Star B

4 Both star A and star B appear to have the same brightness from Earth. **What can you conclude about these stars?**

  F   Star B has a greater absolute magnitude.
  G   The two stars have the same absolute magnitude.
  H   Star B has a greater apparent magnitude.
  J   Star A has a greater apparent magnitude.

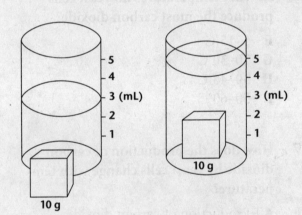

5 Saul has a cubic crystal of a gold-colored mineral. It has a mass of 10 grams. To identify the unknown mineral, Saul needs to determine its density. (Density = mass/volume.) Saul placed the mineral in the right beaker, which contained 3 milliliters of water. **What is the density of the unknown mineral?**

  A   2.0 g/mL
  B   0.5 g/mL
  C   0.2 g/mL
  D   5.0 g/mL

GO ON

Directions: Use the information and the graph below to answer questions 6–7.

A scientist studying yeast, a single-celled fungus, produced the following graph.

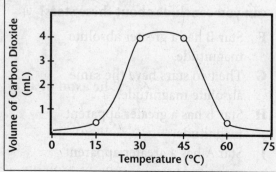

6 At what temperatures do yeast cells produce the most carbon dioxide?

  F 5–15°C

  G 20–30°C

  H 30–45°C

  J 50–60°C

7 How does the production of carbon dioxide by yeast cells change with temperature?

  A Production of carbon dioxide decreases with temperature.

  B Production of carbon dioxide increases with temperature.

  C Production of carbon dioxide decreases as temperature rises, then increases.

  D Production of carbon dioxide increases as temperature rises, then decreases.

8 A river is most likely to have a steep slope and fast-flowing water near its —

  F headwaters

  G flood plain

  H mouth

  J delta

9 Julia is helping her mother put holiday lights on their front porch. She pulled one strand out of the box. When she plugged it in, it did not work. Julia's mother said that one of the bulbs must be burned out. **Which circuit below is most like Julia's holiday lights?**

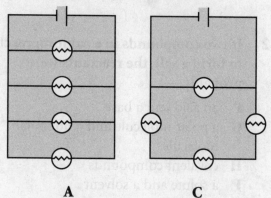

A   C

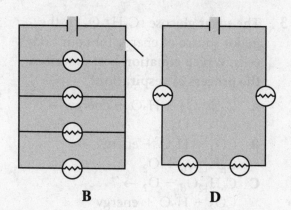

B   D

GO ON

10 Each X on the map below shows where a rabbit was found in the forest. **What is the population density of rabbits in this forest?**

F 20 rabbits per square kilometer

G 4 rabbits per square kilometer

H 5 rabbits per square kilometer

J 10 rabbits per square kilometer

Map of Rabbit Locations

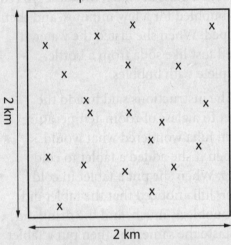

2 km

2 km

11 Which type of volcano usually produces quiet eruptions of flowing lava?

A Shield volcano

B Cinder cone volcano

C Composite volcano

D Dormant volcano

12 Which of the following objects is accelerating?

F A car moving south at 120 km/h

G An airplane moving northwest at 70 m/s

H An elevator moving upward at 5 m/s

J A seat on a Ferris wheel moving in a circle at 5 m/s

Directions: Use the diagram below to answer question 13.

Neuron

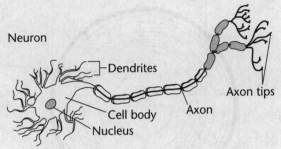

Dendrites

Axon tips

Cell body

Axon

Nucleus

13 What is the function of the axon in a nerve cell?

A Controls all the activities of the neuron

B Receives messages from the axon tips

C Sends messages to the dendrites

D Carries messages away from the cell body

14 What causes surface ocean currents to curve to the right in the Northern Hemisphere?

F The pull of the moon

G Earth's rotation

H The movement of plates under the ocean

J The depth of ocean waters

15 In dry areas, some farmers have water transported to their fields in pipes rather than in open ditches and canals. **How does this save water?**

A Pipes carry less water than ditches and canals.

B Pipes prevent water evaporation.

C Pipes keep the temperature of the water high.

D Pipes prevent water pollution.

GO ON

Youngest   Oldest
Ring   Ring

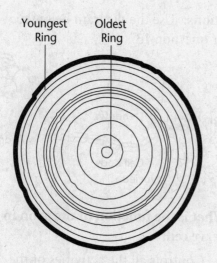

16 The diagram above shows a cross-section of a tree trunk. **What can you infer from this diagram?**

F The tree is growing in a desert.
G A drought occurred between four and seven years ago.
H A drought occurred during the first three years of the tree's life.
J A drought has occurred during the last three years.

17 Some of the sun's energy is absorbed by Earth's surface and released back into the atmosphere as —

A infrared radiation
B greenhouse gases
C ultraviolet light
D visible light

18 Which organism has a segmented body and a closed circulatory system?

F Earthworm
G Sponge
H Crayfish
J Spider

Directions: Use the information given below to answer question 19.

While shopping with her mother, Julia bought a new product that claimed to make instant fruit-flavored soda in a glass of water. The instructions said to add one tablet to a glass of room-temperature water. When Julia put a tablet in a glass of water, the tablet fizzed and bubbled for a few minutes, and then stopped. When she tasted the water, it tasted just like soda from a bottle, complete with bubbles.

The instructions said to add the tablet to a glass of room-temperature water. Julia wondered what would happen if she added a tablet to cold water. When she put a tablet in cold water, Julia noticed that the tablet did not bubble as much, and the drink did not taste the same. She then put a tablet in a glass of hot water. The tablet bubbled much faster, spilling soda over the edge of the glass.

19 What statement best explains what happened when Julia put the tablets in hot and cold water?

A The different temperatures caused different chemical reactions.
B The different temperatures affected the rate of the chemical reaction.
C The different temperatures had no affect on the chemical reaction.
D The chemical reaction only worked in room-temperature water.

GO ON

SAT9 PREP GRADE 7 PRACTICE TEST (continued)

20 Which of these arthropods is *not* an arachnid?

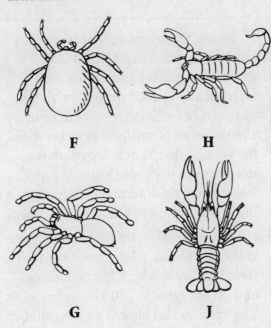

F   H

G   J

21 Which part of the sun is visible during a total solar eclipse?

   A The corona
   B The photosphere
   C Sunspots
   D The chromosphere

22 Which of the following occurs because of inertia?

   F A ball falls to the ground after it is thrown.
   G A helium balloon rises into the sky when it is released.
   H People in a car that stops suddenly continue to move forward unless they are wearing seat belts.
   J A basketball exerts a force on the floor when it bounces, and the floor exerts an equal but opposite force on the basketball.

23 A scientist planted two morning glory vines. He put a stake near the first vine. The first vine grew upward, coiling around the stake, while the second vine grew low to the ground. **Why did only the first vine grow upward?**

   A It responded positively to the stimulus of touching the stake.
   B It responded more strongly to light than the second vine.
   C It responded less strongly to gravity than the second vine.
   D It responded negatively to the stimulus of touching the ground.

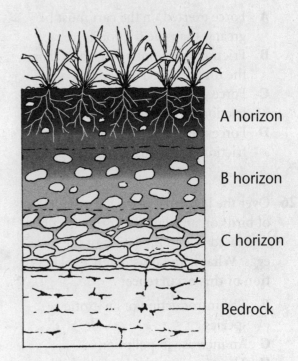

A horizon

B horizon

C horizon

Bedrock

24 Which soil layer is also called subsoil?

   F Bedrock
   G C horizon
   H B horizon
   J A horizon

Name _____ Date _____ Class _____

SAT9 PREP GRADE 7 PRACTICE TEST *(continued)*

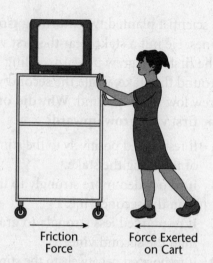

Friction Force | Force Exerted on Cart

25 **Which of the following must be true in order for the cart to move?**

A Force exerted on the cart must be greater than the friction force.

B Friction force must be greater than the force exerted on the cart.

C Force exerted on the cart and the friction force must be equal.

D Force exerted on the cart and the friction force must equal zero.

26 Over the last three years, the population of birds on an island has dramatically decreased due to predation of the birds' eggs. **What is the most likely explanation of this occurrence?**

F The introduction of an exotic species

G An increase in pollution

H The capture and sale of the birds as pets

J Destruction of the birds' habitat

Directions: Use the information given below to answer questions 27–29.

> Mount St. Helens in Washington is a tall, steep volcano that formed from many layers of lava alternating with layers of ash. It stood quietly for almost 123 years before it began to rumble in 1980. A series of small earthquakes shook the volcano that March. A part of its northeastern slope also began to bulge. The volcano finally erupted on May 18. It blew away 400 meters of its top.
>
> Ash, gas, and steam roared out of the volcano. The fiery, hot wind blew down trees like toothpicks. It burned leaves and other vegetation 20 kilometers away. The volcano also blasted an ash cloud 25 kilometers into the atmosphere. The cloud drifted hundreds of kilometers to the east, blocking the sun at noon and dumping a thick carpet of ash on several northwestern states.

27 **Which type of volcano is Mount St. Helens?**

A Composite volcano

B Fire volcano

C Cinder cone volcano

D Shield volcano

GO ON

SAT9 PREP GRADE 7 PRACTICE TEST (continued)

28 Volcanic ash clouds often change climate temporarily, making it colder. **Why does this change occur?**

F The ash clouds block the sun's radiation.

G The ash clouds create more oxygen in the atmosphere.

H The ash clouds alter Earth's rotation.

J The ash clouds absorb heat from Earth.

29 What instrument could geologists have used to measure slight changes in the volcano's surface elevation?

A Sonar

B Seismometer

C Tiltmeter

D Mass spectrometer

 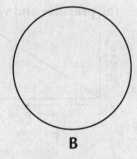

A   B

30 Two balls, A and B, were thrown from a building at the same time. Ball A hit the ground after 2 seconds. **Assuming that there is no air resistance, when did ball B hit the ground?**

F At the same time as ball A

G After ball A

H Before ball A

J It cannot be determined unless the masses of the balls are known.

31 What kind of orbit allows a satellite to remain over one point on Earth?

A Circular

B Geosynchronous

C Elliptical

D High

32 Which of the following organisms existed during the Paleozoic Era?

F   H

G   J

33 Suppose the magnet in the picture were cut in half along the dotted line. **What would the result be?**

A Two magnets would be formed, each with a north and south pole.

B The two pieces would not be magnets.

C Only one piece would be magnetic.

D Two magnets would be formed, one with only a north pole and one with only a south pole.

GO ON

SAT9 PREP GRADE 7 PRACTICE TEST (continued)

34 A clone is an organism that is —

F a product of selective breeding
G genetically identical to the organism from which it was produced
H a cross between two genetically different individuals
J produced through the process of genetic engineering

35 Why can X-rays and gamma rays penetrate most matter, when other electromagnetic waves cannot?

A X-rays and gamma rays have higher frequencies and more energy than other electromagnetic waves.
B X-rays and gamma rays have lower frequencies and more energy than other electromagnetic waves.
C X-rays and gamma rays have longer wavelengths and less energy than other electromagnetic waves.
D X-rays and gamma rays have lower frequencies and less energy than other electromagnetic waves.

36 Which of the following is *not* an abiotic factor in an ecosystem?

F The yearly rainfall
G The number of plants
H The average temperature
J The amount of oxygen in the water

37 An infectious disease is caused by —

A a pathogen
B defective genes
C toxins
D missing chromosomes

38 A solute was added to a solvent and mixed well. Some of the solute fell to the bottom of the container. **Which best explains why all of the solute did not dissolve?**

F The solution was unsaturated.
G The solute was not soluble in the solvent.
H The solution was heated to increase solubility.
J The solution became saturated.

39 What happens when your trachea is irritated by foreign particles?

A You sneeze.   C You cough.
B You hiccup.   D You blink.

40 If temperature is constant, which graph shows the relationship between the pressure and volume of a gas?

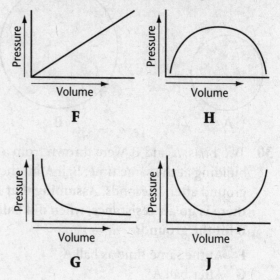

STOP

1 Homeostasis refers to an organism's ability to —

A maintain stable internal conditions
B compete for living space
C dissolve chemicals
D obtain energy

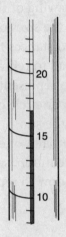

2 What is the temperature on the Celsius thermometer shown above?

J 0.6°C   L 2°C
K 1.2°C   M 6°C

3 What is the result when chemical bonds break and new bonds form?

A A physical change occurs.
B A chemical reaction occurs.
C Matter is destroyed.
D Surface area increases.

4 How does a grasshopper get oxygen?

J Through gills
K Through a system of tubes
L Through its skin
M By breathing through its mouth

5 The buildup of charges on an object is called —

A static discharge
B static electricity
C positive charge
D negative charge

6 In conservation plowing, why are dead weeds and stalks of the previous year's crop left in the ground?

J To keep the soil from becoming too fertile
K To reduce the amount of seed needed for the next year's crop
L To retain moisture and hold the soil in place
M To keep more organisms out of the soil

7 What happens when two forces act in the same direction?

A They cancel each other out.
B The stronger one prevails.
C They add together.
D Their sum divided by two is the total force.

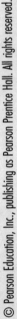
GO ON

Rivers and Streams

8 **Which of the labeled features represents an oxbow lake?**

J B   L E
K D   M F

9 **What happens during respiration?**

A Oxygen is released into the air.
B Glucose is broken down, releasing energy.
C Carbohydrates are released into the bloodstream.
D Water and carbon dioxide are converted into energy.

10 **The ideal mechanical advantage of a wheel and axle is equal to the —**

J radius of the wheel divided by the radius of the axle
K radius of the axle divided by the radius of the wheel
L radius of the wheel divided by the length of the axle
M length of the axle divided by the radius of the wheel

11 **Which of the following would be a good model to demonstrate a lunar eclipse?**

A A large ball of clay to represent Earth, a small ball of clay to represent the moon, and a flashlight to represent the sun
B A scale drawing of the solar system, including the sizes of the planets and their distances from the sun
C A basketball to represent Earth, a baseball to represent the moon, and a large paper circle on the wall to represent the sun
D Two basketballs, one for Earth and one for the moon, set up facing a sunlit window to represent the sun

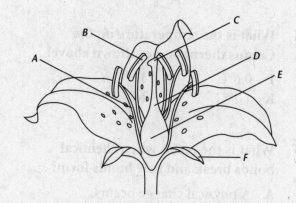

12 **Which of these structures are female reproductive structures?**

J A and B
K B and C
L E and F
M C, D, and E

GO ON

ITBS PREP GRADE 7 PRACTICE TEST (*continued*)

13 Ozone is —

A a form of oxygen with three oxygen atoms in each molecule

B a form of nitrogen with three oxygen atoms in each molecule

C a form of oxygen with two oxygen atoms in each molecule

D a form of nitrogen with two oxygen atoms in each molecule

14 The type of graph that shows data as parts or percentages of a whole is called a —

J bar graph
K circle graph
L data table
M line graph

15 A characteristic property that can help tell similar liquids apart is —

A hardness
B melting point
C boiling point
D smell

16 Which of the following is the best description of adolescence?

J The stage when children become adults physically and mentally
K The stage when individuals first produce hormones
L The stage that's the same as puberty
M The stage when people have "growing pains"

17 Materials that allow the charges of an electric current to move freely through them are called —

A insulators
B conductors
C resistors
D magnets

18 The behaviors and physical characteristics of species that allow them to live successfully in their environment are called —

J habitats
K limiting factors
L biotic factors
M adaptations

19 Which of the following is an example of a correctly written, testable hypothesis?

A People should taste this new health food and see whether it makes them stronger.

B When dog owners don't feed their puppies Brand A food, the puppies do not grow properly.

C If Frederico had added the leaves to the compost pile last year, he wouldn't have to buy organic fertilizer now.

D If it is dark, then an owl will find a mouse by the sound the mouse makes.

GO ON

ITBS PREP GRADE 7 PRACTICE TEST *(continued)*

20 During which phase of the moon are the tides highest?

J

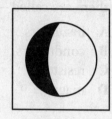

L

K

M

21 Which of the following tools would you use to measure the length of a piece of metal wire about the size of a paper clip?

  A A meter stick calibrated in centimeters

  B A metric ruler calibrated in millimeters

  C A triple-beam balance calibrated in grams

  D A microscope with a ruler calibrated in microns

22 Which of the following levers is the same class as a pair of scissors?

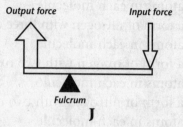

J

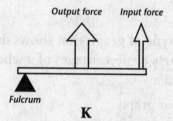

K

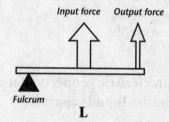

L

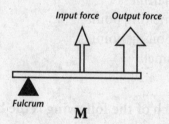

M

23 What does the backbone protect in a vertebrate?

  A Its heart and lungs

  B Its notochord

  C Its spinal cord

  D Its pharyngeal cord

GO ON

ITBS PREP GRADE 7 PRACTICE TEST (continued)

24 The energy that produces ocean waves comes from —

J   the rise and fall of the tides
K   rivers flowing into the ocean
L   wind blowing across the water's surface
M   rock falling into the ocean along the shore

25 You are more likely to see a lunar eclipse than a solar eclipse because —

A   the moon's shadow covers all of Earth during a solar eclipse
B   new moon phases occur less often than full moon phases
C   only people on the daytime side of Earth can see a solar eclipse
D   you must be in the moon's shadow to see a solar eclipse

26 Which of the following is a qualitative observation?

J   There are 21 students in the room.
K   The classroom walls are yellow.
L   The chalkboard is 1 meter high and 2 meters wide.
M   Sixteen students were present for roll call, and five other students arrived afterward.

27 Which of the following is a name for the body's reaction to stress?

A   Reaction response
B   Stimulus response
C   Fight-or-flight response
D   Reasonable response

28 How can you increase the momentum of an object?

J   By decreasing its velocity
K   By increasing its mass
L   By increasing its friction
M   By decreasing its acceleration

29 Hibernation gives animals which of the following benefits?

A   Protection from harsh weather
B   Protection from dry weather
C   The ability to raise their young in safety
D   An opportunity to attract mates

30 The conversion of thermal energy into mechanical energy requires a —

J   thermometer
K   heat engine
L   vaporizer
M   thermostat

31 Landslides, mudflows, slump, and creep are all examples of —

A   mechanical weathering
B   runoff
C   mass movement
D   soil formation

GO ON

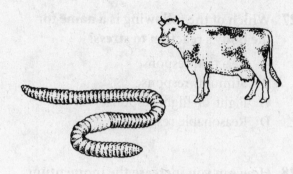

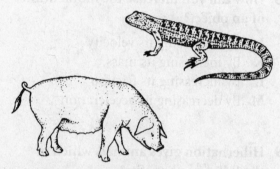

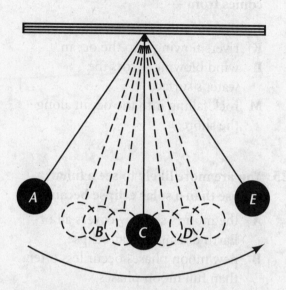

Energy of a Pendulum

32 **Which of the following classification systems would be helpful in classifying these organisms?**

  J Live on water/live on land
  K Have feathers/have hair
  L Have wings/no wings
  M Have legs/no legs

33 **Which of the following statements would belong in the conclusions section of a lab report?**

  A Water that contains sugar freezes at a lower temperature than water without sugar.
  B Why doesn't the ocean water have ice on it when the lake does?
  C 2 plastic containers, tap water, 15 grams of sugar, 2 wooden stirrers, a freezer
  D If water contains sugar, then it will freeze at a lower temperature than fresh water.

34 **Which letters represent the positions of maximum potential energy of the pendulum?**

  J A and B
  K C and D
  L D and E
  M A and E

35 **The layer in our atmosphere in which weather occurs is the —**

  A troposphere
  B stratosphere
  C mesosphere
  D exosphere

36 **What makes a leaf appear green?**

  J Accessory pigments
  K Chlorophyll
  L Vascular tissue
  M Cuticle

GO ON

37 Earth has seasons because —

   A Earth rotates on its axis

   B the distance between Earth and the sun changes

   C Earth's axis is tilted as it moves around the sun

   D the temperature of the sun changes

38 A geologist finds deep gouges and scratches on bedrock in an area once covered by a glacier. **These scratches are evidence of the type of erosion called —**

   J creep

   K mass movement

   L abrasion

   M plucking

39 In an energy pyramid, which level has the most available energy?

   A Producer level

   B First-level consumer level

   C Second-level consumer level

   D Third-level consumer level

40 Plowing removed the grass from the Great Plains and exposed the soil. **What effect did this have when a drought struck the Great Plains during the 1930s?**

   J It had no effect.

   K It reduced the soil's fertility.

   L It helped to cause the Dust Bowl.

   M It prevented sod from developing.

41 An example of something that stores chemical energy is —

   A lightning

   B a microwave

   C a match

   D the sun

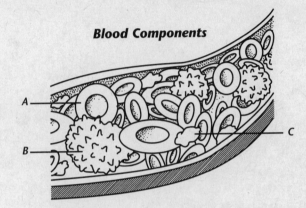

Blood Components

42 Which of these blood components fight(s) disease?

   J A

   K B

   L C

   M B and C

STOP

1 A device that is twice as powerful as another can do the same amount of work in —

A half the time
B twice the time
C one third the time
D the same amount of time

2 Because the moon rotates once for each revolution around Earth —

F you see some phases more than others
G a different side of the moon faces Earth each day
H you never see the far side of the moon
J the far side of the moon is visible only during the full moon phase

3 Which of the following might be the materials list for an experiment?

A Data tables and graphs
B Meters, liters, and kilograms
C Plastic containers, soil, water, thermometers, and plants
D Temperature, light, and time

Periodic Table of the Elements (Top Section)

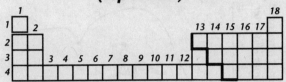

4 What name is given to the elements in Groups 3 through 12?

F Transition metals
G Alkali metals
H Alkaline earth metals
J Metal alloys

5 What causes blood pressure?

A The force with which the ventricles contract
B The rate at which blood flows through the heart
C The speed at which oxygen is returned to blood in the lungs
D The strength of the muscles in the walls of the capillaries

6 The most important factors in determining the rate of weathering are —

F carbon dioxide and acid rain
G abrasion and acids from plant roots
H animal actions and oxygen
J rock type and climate

GO ON

Pheasant Population

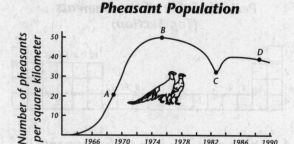

7 **What are some possible explanations for the change in pheasant population between Point B and Point C?**

A   A natural disaster

B   An excess of food for the population

C   Human interactions causing fewer deaths

D   A lack of nesting space causing more births

8 **Which of the following is a characteristic property of ionic compounds?**

F   They have low melting points.

G   They have low boiling points.

H   They form crystals with characteristic shapes.

J   They contain no charged particles.

9 You are planning an experiment to find out whether the rate at which water freezes depends on the shape of its container. You choose a short square container and a tall cylindrical container. **Which of the following is *not* a variable in the experiment?**

A   The size of each container

B   The starting temperature of the water

C   The volume of water in each container

D   The material of the containers

10 **Day and night are caused by —**

F   the tilt of Earth's axis

G   Earth's revolution around the sun

H   eclipses

J   Earth's rotation on its axis

11 **A species that influences the survival of many other species in an ecosystem is called a(n) —**

A   niche species

B   extinct species

C   keystone species

D   endangered species

GO ON

TERRANOVA PREP GRADE 7 PRACTICE TEST (continued)

12 In which container is the air pressure inside the glass tube the greatest?

Balanced Pressures

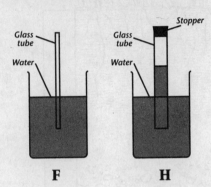

F   H

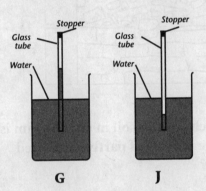

G   J

13 An organized arrangement of information in labeled rows and columns is called a —

 A bar graph
 B line graph
 C circle graph
 D data table

14 Glaciers can form only when —

 F there is an ice age
 G there is a U-shaped valley in the mountains
 H the amount of snow exceeds the amount of rain
 J more snow falls than melts each year

15 Which process takes place in the large intestine?

 A Water is added to undigested food.
 B Water is absorbed from undigested food.
 C Digested nutrients are absorbed through the villi.
 D Enzymes are added to complete chemical digestion.

16 What is the total magnification of a microscope with two lenses when one lens has a magnification of 15 and the other lens has a magnification of 30?

 F $15\times$
 G $30\times$
 H $45\times$
 J $450\times$

GO ON

17 How is a solute different from a solvent in a solution?

  A The solute is present in a smaller amount.

  B The solute is present in a greater amount.

  C The solute is a solid and the solvent is a liquid.

  D The solute is a liquid and the solvent is a gas.

18 Which of the following statements is a quantitative observation?

  F There's an empty aquarium tank in the classroom.

  G The tank used to contain live fish.

  H The tank is waterproof.

  J The tank is 50 cm long, 30 cm wide, and 18 cm deep.

19 How do breathing passages help keep pathogens out of the body?

  A Chemicals kill some pathogens.

  B Mucus and cilia trap pathogens.

  C Phagocytes in the breathing passages destroy pathogens.

  D The passages produce antibodies that kill pathogens.

Soil Development

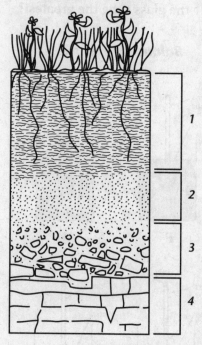

20 Which layer of soil in the diagram is made up only of partly weathered rock?

  F 1

  G 2

  H 3

  J 4

21 Which of the following could be considered an inclined plane wrapped around a cylinder?

  A Lever

  B Screw

  C Wheel and axle

  D Pulley

GO ON

22 How many meters are in 3 kilometers?

  F 0.3 m

  G 30 m

  H 300 m

  J 3000 m

Coastal Landforms

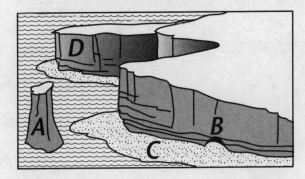

23 Which of these coastal landforms is the result of deposition?

  A A

  B B

  C C

  D D

24 The way the endocrine system maintains homeostasis is often compared to a —

  F violent thunderstorm that startles people and increases their heartbeat

  G heating system that turns a furnace on and off to control a room's temperature

  H monthly cycle that releases an egg from an ovary

  J period of human development that takes about nine months to be completed

25 Which of the following is a correctly written, testable hypothesis?

  A If I give my plants fertilizer, then they will grow as big as my neighbor's plants.

  B If I get lucky, my plants will grow bigger.

  C My plants aren't growing bigger because I don't water them enough.

  D My neighbor's yard gets more sun than mine does.

26 The pH scale measures —

  F the strength of an acid

  G the strength of hydrogen ions

  H the concentration of hydrogen ions

  J the concentration of an acid

27 The series of changes that occurs after a disturbance in an existing ecosystem is called —

  A primary succession

  B secondary succession

  C disturbance succession

  D pioneer succession

GO ON

28 How would a fast-flowing river be most likely to move sand-sized particles of sediment?

  F It would carry them suspended in the water.

  G It would dissolve them completely in solution.

  H It would push or slide them along the streambed.

  J It would deposit them along its banks.

29 The thick column of nerve tissue that links the brain to most of the nerves in the peripheral nervous system is the —

  A brain

  B spinal cord

  C cerebellum

  D cornea

30 When constructing a line graph, what category should be used to label the horizontal axis?

  F The manipulated variable

  G The responding variable

  H The controlled variable

  J The relationship between the variables

31 Two figure skaters who push off each other will move at the same speed if —

  A they push with the same force

  B the ice does not cause any friction

  C there is no air resistance

  D they have the same mass

32 Based on the illustration above, which of the following statements is an unreasonable inference?

  F The antelope are watching for predators.

  G The cattle and antelope do not attack each other.

  H The grass is food for the cattle and antelope.

  J Most of the grass in this area is eaten by the cattle.

GO ON

TERRANOVA PREP GRADE 7 PRACTICE TEST *(continued)*

33 Which joint provides the greatest range of movement?

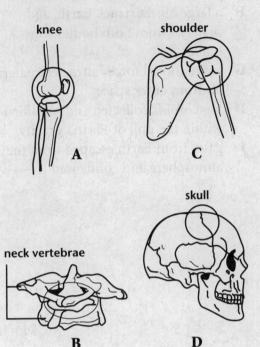

knee

shoulder

A

C

neck vertebrae

skull

B

D

34 If there is already a slight depression in the ground, wind erosion may form a larger, bowl-shaped hollow called a —

F kettle
G desert pavement
H prairie pothole
J blowout

35 For work to be done on an object, such as pushing a child on a swing —

A some force need only be exerted on the object
B the object must move some distance as a result of a force
C the object must move, whether or not a force is exerted on it
D the object must move a distance equal to the amount of force exerted on it

36 What function do the kidneys perform?

F Eliminate carbon dioxide
G Supply oxygen to body cells
H Eliminate urea and excess water
J Play a role in gas exchange

37 An equinox occurs when —

A neither end of Earth's axis is tilted toward or away from the sun
B the north end of Earth's axis is tilted away from the sun
C the north end of Earth's axis is tilted toward the sun
D Earth's axis is parallel to the sun's rays

GO ON

TERRANOVA PREP GRADE 7 PRACTICE TEST *(continued)*

38 Kinetic energy increases as —

    F mass increases and velocity decreases

    G mass decreases and velocity increases

    H both mass and velocity increase

    J both mass and velocity decrease

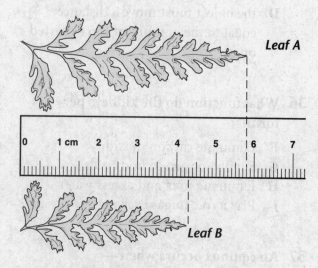

39 How many centimeters longer is Leaf A than Leaf B?

    A 5.8 cm

    B 4.3 cm

    C 2.7 cm

    D 1.5 cm

40 Scientists think the moon was formed when —

    F a large object struck Earth, and material from both bodies combined

    G gravitational forces attracted materials from outer space

    H meteoroids collected and solidified within the pull of Earth's gravity

    J gases from Earth escaped from the atmosphere and condensed

STOP

SAT9 PREP   **GRADE 8 PRACTICE TEST**

1 **What type of galaxy is shown in the picture?**

  A Nebula

  B Irregular

  C Elliptical

  D Spiral

2 **Which element has the ability to form straight chains, branched chains, and rings because its atoms can form four covalent bonds?**

  F Carbon

  G Hydrogen

  H Nitrogen

  J Oxygen

3 Hot columns of mantle material slowly rise, cool, and sink through Earth's asthenosphere. **This type of heat transfer is called —**

  A subduction

  B radiation

  C conduction

  D convection

Directions: Use the information given below to answer questions 4–6.

> A dog breeder has begun to raise Labrador retrievers. So far, she hasn't been able to predict the color of the puppies that she breeds. She does not know that dark fur (D) is dominant over yellow fur (d).
>
> When the breeder crossed a yellow female Labrador retriever with a male Labrador with dark fur, she expected half of the puppies to be yellow and half to be dark. However, in a litter of 8 puppies, all had dark fur. The breeder next crossed the same yellow female with a different dark male. This time, half of the puppies were yellow and half were dark.

4 **Which letters represent the most probable genotype of the second male?**

  F Dd

  G DD

  H DO

  J dd

5 **How can the woman breed a litter of all yellow puppies?**

  A By making sure that either the mother or the father is yellow

  B By making sure that both the mother and the father are yellow

  C By making sure that at least one of the grandparents is yellow

  D She cannot breed a yellow litter since yellow fur is recessive.

GO ON

6 The breeder is going to cross two dark Labradors. One is homozygous and the other is heterozygous. **Predict what percentage of the puppies will be yellow.**

  F 0
  G 25
  H 50
  J 75

Directions: Use the diagram below to answer questions 7–8.

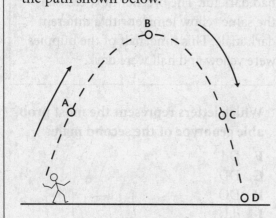

A ball is thrown into the air and follows the path shown below.

7 At which point is the ball's potential energy greatest?

  A A
  B B
  C C
  D D

8 At which point is the ball's kinetic energy greatest?

  F A
  G B
  H C
  J D

Directions: Use the diagram below to answer questions 9–10.

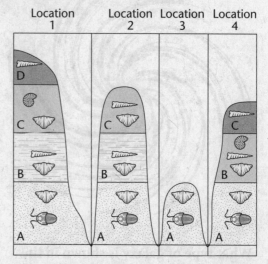

Location 1   Location 2   Location 3   Location 4

9 Each layer belongs to one time period. **At location 2, index fossils are found —**

  A only in layer A
  B only in layer C
  C in layers A and B
  D in layers B and C

10 A geologist collected the following index fossil from layer B at location 4. **What can the geologist infer?**

  F Layer C at location 1 is older than layer B at location 4.
  G Layer C at location 1 is younger than layer B at location 4.
  H Layer C at location 1 is about the same age as layer B at location 4.
  J The relative age of layer C at location 1 cannot be determined.

GO ON

Directions: Use the periodic table to answer questions 11–12.

11 Which line on the periodic table separates the metals from the non-metals and metalloids?

   A I
   B II
   C III
   D IV

12 Where on the periodic table are the most reactive metals found?

   F Right
   G Middle
   H Bottom
   J Left

13 The scientific name for a house cat is *Felis domesticus.* **Felis** is the name of the —

   A family
   B genus
   C species
   D variety

14 A solution of soapy water has a slippery feel, turns red litmus paper blue, and has a pH of 8.5. **The soapy water is best described as a(n) —**

   F neutral solution
   G acidic solution
   H corrosive solution
   J basic solution

15 The sun appears to move across the sky each day because —

   A the sun is moving faster than Earth
   B our reference point, the sun, is accelerating
   C we assume that our reference point, Earth, is not moving
   D the sun is orbiting Earth

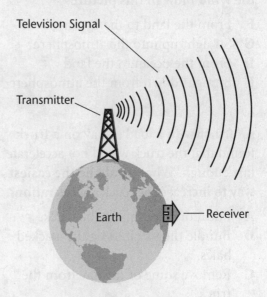

16 What could help the home in the picture receive the television signal?

   F A tall antenna
   G A more powerful transmitter
   H A satellite
   J A new television

GO ON

17 Mammals that lay eggs are called —

A marsupials
B monotremes
C placental mammals
D flying mammals

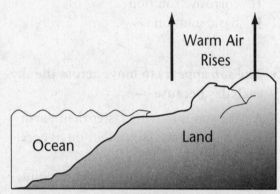

Warm Air Rises

Ocean

Land

18 During the day, the land warms up faster than the ocean. **Which way will the wind blow in this picture?**

F From the land to the ocean
G Straight up into the atmosphere
H From the ocean to the land
J Straight down from the atmosphere

19 A farmer with a load of hay on a truck found that the truck would not accelerate fast enough. **What would be the easiest way to increase the truck's acceleration?**

A Put more gasoline in the truck.
B Bundle the hay into tightly-packed bales.
C Remove some of the hay from the truck.
D Put more hay on the truck.

Directions: Use the information given below to answer questions 20–21.

Samantha repeated Redi's experiment for a spontaneous generation project. She placed meat in two identical jars. She covered one jar with plastic wrap. She left the other uncovered. After a few days, Samantha observed young flies (maggots) on the meat in the open jar. There were no flies in the covered jar.

20 What was Samantha trying to discover?

F Does decaying meat produce maggots?
G Do maggots prefer one type of meat to another?
H Does the appearance of maggots depend on temperature?
J Does plastic wrap prevent meat from spoiling?

21 What conclusion should Samantha have reached?

A Meat will not decay if it is covered.
B Decaying meat produces maggots.
C Decaying meat does not produce maggots.
D Maggots live in meat and grow as the meat ages.

22 When the largest stars die, they first become supernovas, and then they become —

F comets
G black holes
H white dwarfs
J protostars

GO ON

SAT9 PREP GRADE 8 PRACTICE TEST (continued)

Directions: Use the information given below to answer questions 23–25.

> Jenny's family had a new home built on 20 acres of land that they bought in the country. The family decided that their new home should get its energy from more than one source.
>
> The first source of energy the family had installed was electricity from the local power company. Then they added a propane tank to supply gas for cooking. They had solar panels put on their roof to help heat their hot water. The many windows on the south side of the house let in sunlight. The sunlight would help warm the house in the winter. They also bought a wood burning stove to use as the main source of heat for the house.
>
> Because they lived in the country, the family's water came from a well. Instead of putting an electric pump in the well, they installed a windmill. The windmill pumped water from the well into a water tower. Gravity then carried the water through pipes into their home.

23 The main source of heat in Jenny's house uses a renewable resource. **What is that resource?**

   A Solar energy
   B Biomass fuel
   C Wind energy
   D Geothermal energy

24 What two features of Jenny's home are designed to trap solar energy?

   F The water tower and the windmill
   G Panels on the roof and the water tower
   H The propane tank and the stove
   J The windows and panels on the roof

25 What would be the most likely effect on Jenny's family if there were little or no wind for a period of ten days?

   A They would not be able to use electrical appliances.
   B They would have to burn more wood to keep their house warm.
   C They would have to find another source of water.
   D They would have to take cold showers.

26 What might be the most serious effect of placing a factory in the location shown below?

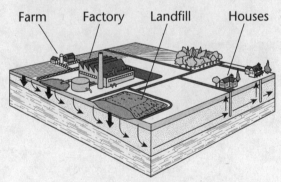

Farm   Factory   Landfill   Houses

   F Groundwater might be used up too quickly.
   G Pollution from the factory could seep into groundwater.
   H Groundwater could become salt water.
   J Groundwater could seep into the factory.

GO ON

SAT9 PREP GRADE 8 PRACTICE TEST (continued)

Directions: The table below shows approximate amounts of gases inhaled and exhaled by humans. Use the table to answer question 27.

Gases in Inhaled and Exhaled Air

Gas	Inhaled Air	Exhaled Air
Nitrogen	78%	78%
Oxygen	21%	16%
Carbon dioxide	0.03%	4%

27 **What conclusion can you draw from this data?**

  A Inhaled air contains less oxygen and more carbon dioxide than exhaled air.

  B Inhaled air contains more oxygen and less carbon dioxide than exhaled air.

  C Inhaled air contains more oxygen and more carbon dioxide than exhaled air.

  D Inhaled air contains the same amount of nitrogen and carbon dioxide as exhaled air.

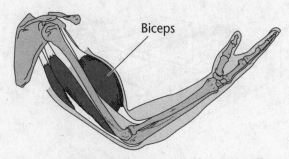

Biceps

28 **Why is the biceps classified as a skeletal muscle?**

  F It is attached to bones and is used to move them.

  G It reacts and tires slowly.

  H Its contractions are involuntary.

  J It is found in internal organs.

29 **Coarse-grained igneous rocks, such as granite, —**

  A form from molten material at mid-ocean ridges

  B cool quickly from lava at Earth's surface

  C cool slowly from magma deep within Earth

  D form in shield volcanoes

$$\left(\begin{matrix} H & H & H & H & H & H & H & H \\ | & | & | & | & | & | & | & | \\ C\!-\!C\!-\!C\!-\!C\!-\!C\!-\!C\!-\!C\!-\!C \\ | & | & | & | & | & | & | & | \\ H & H & H & H & H & H & H & H \end{matrix}\right)_n$$

30 This diagram shows only a small portion of this molecule in which —CH_2— repeats over and over. **What kind of molecule is it?**

  F A polymer   **H** A polar molecule

  G An ion   **J** A salt molecule

31 **What is the function of a red blood cell?**

  A To transport white blood cells

  B To ward off infection

  C To transport carbon dioxide and oxygen

  D To aid in blood clotting

32 **What is a river's watershed?**

  F The area of land that supplies water to a river system

  G A natural dam across a river

  H The early stage of a pond formed by a river

  J The point where a river flows into another body of water

GO ON

SAT9 PREP GRADE 8 PRACTICE TEST *(continued)*

33 Besides water vapor, what must be present for clouds to form?

A Sunlight
B A strong wind
C Particles of salt, dust, or smoke
D Dew

Directions: Use the information given below to answer question 34.

Nutrition Facts

Serving Size	1 cup (30 g)
Servings Per Container	About 10

Amount Per Serving

Calories 110	Calories from Fat 15

	% Daily Value*
Total Fat 2 g	**3%**
Saturated Fat 0 g	**0%**
Cholesterol 0 mg	**0%**
Sodium 280 mg	**12%**
Total Carbohydrates 22 g	**7%**
Dietary Fiber 3 g	**12%**
Sugars 1 g	
Protein 3 g	

Vitamin A	10%	·	Vitamin C	20%
Calcium	4%	·	Iron	45%

* Percent Daily Values are based on a 2,000 Calorie diet. Your daily values may be higher or lower depending on your caloric needs.

34 How much unsaturated fat does each serving of this food contain?

F 0 g
G 1 g
H 2 g
J 3 g

35 The rate of chemical weathering would most likely be the highest in —

A a hot and wet climate such as a tropical rain forest near the equator
B a hot and dry climate such as a desert
C a cool and wet climate such as a coniferous forest
D a cool and dry climate such as a tundra

36 Which of the following is *not* recycled in an ecosystem?

F Water
G Nitrogen
H Oxygen
J Energy

37 The illustration below shows the furrows of a farmer's field. **What method has this farmer used to prevent erosion?**

A Conservation plowing
B Sod irrigation
C Overgrazing
D Contour plowing

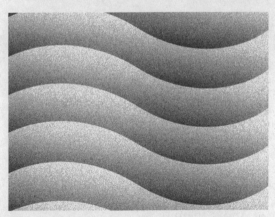

GO ON

38 **What must happen for water to change state?**

F   It must maintain the same energy level.

G   It must absorb solar energy.

H   It must absorb or release energy.

J   Its temperature must decrease.

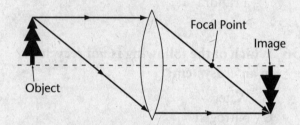

39 **What type of image is being produced by the lens?**

A   Virtual, because the image and the object are on opposite sides of the lens

B   Virtual, because the focal point is between the lens and the image

C   Real, because the image and the object are the same size

D   Real, because the image is upside down

40 **Arachnids, centipedes, millipedes, and insects are types of —**

F   arthropods

G   mollusks

H   echinoderms

J   amphibians

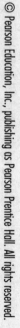

1 Most geologists rejected Alfred Wegener's idea of continental drift because —

  A they were afraid of a new idea
  B Wegener was interested in what Earth was like millions of years ago
  C Wegener used several different types of evidence to support his hypothesis
  D Wegener could not identify a force that could move the continents

2 To determine the acceleration rate of an object, you must calculate the change in velocity during each unit of —

  J speed
  K time
  L motion
  M deceleration

3 All plants are —

  A autotrophs
  B unicellular
  C heterotrophs
  D prokaryotes

4 How does a microscope lens work?

  J Each concave lens bends light to make the object appear larger.
  K Each convex lens bends light to make the object appear larger.
  L Each convex lens bends light to make the object become larger.
  M The reflection of each concave lens makes the object appear larger.

Layers of the Atmosphere

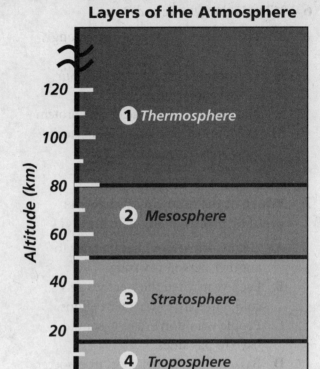

5 What is the main feature of the atmospheric layer labeled 3?

  A It is where Earth's weather occurs.
  B It contains the ozone layer, which absorbs ultraviolet radiation from the sun.
  C It protects Earth's surface from being hit by meteoroids.
  D It contains ions that bounce radio waves back to Earth's surface.

GO ON

6 **What is the genetic code?**

J The order of nitrogen bases along a gene

K The number of nitrogen bases in a DNA molecule

L The order of amino acids in a protein

M The number of guanine and cytosine bases in a chromosome

7 **Which of the following statements could be investigated scientifically?**

A Taking something that belongs to another person is wrong.

B Each year when the weather gets cold, birds fly to warmer regions.

C People who don't recycle should have to pay fines.

D Basketball is a better sport than soccer.

8 **How are elliptical galaxies and spiral galaxies different?**

J Elliptical galaxies have almost no gas or dust.

K Elliptical galaxies vary more in shape than spiral galaxies.

L Spiral galaxies have almost no gas or dust.

M Spiral galaxies contain only old stars.

9 **The first species to populate an area where primary succession is taking place are called —**

A secondary species

B primary species

C pioneer species

D succession species

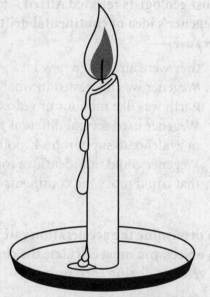

10 The flame from the candle gives off black smoke. **What kind of change is occurring?**

J Precipitation

K Condensation

L Chemical change

M Physical change

11 **When a person's body needs water, the brain helps maintain homeostasis by sending signals that make the person —**

A feel thirsty

B perspire

C put on a sweater

D feel tired

GO ON

ITBS PREP GRADE 8 PRACTICE TEST *(continued)*

12 When two or more substances combine to make a more complex compound, the process is called a —

   J decomposition reaction
   K replacement reaction
   L precipitate reaction
   M synthesis reaction

Cell Structures

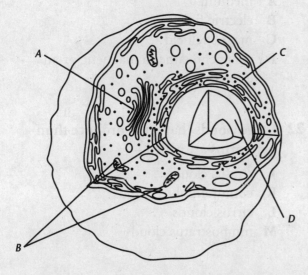

13 What is the function of the structure labeled A?

   A Directs the activities of the cell
   B Produces most of the energy the cell needs
   C Packages proteins and distributes them to other parts of the cell
   D Produces proteins

14 Which of the following statements is an example of a correctly written, testable hypothesis?

   J Does handling toads cause warts?
   K If a truck is heavily loaded, then it will use more gasoline than an empty truck.
   L Exercising for five minutes will increase my heart rate.
   M If water contains salt, then it will be easier to swim in than fresh water.

15 Any force that causes an object to move in a circle is called a(n) —

   A balanced force
   B unbalanced force
   C gravitational force
   D centripetal force

16 Nutritionists place certain foods at the top of the Food Guide Pyramid to indicate that —

   J foods from this group should be included with every meal
   K people should make most of their food choices from this group
   L people should eat very small amounts from this group
   M these foods are not easily digested

GO ON

The Rock Cycle

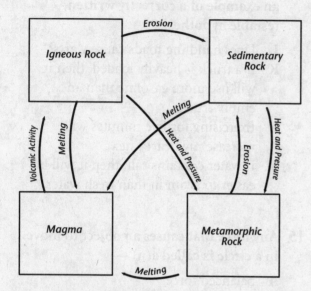

17 What step in the rock cycle helps sedimentary rock form?

A Melting
B Erosion
C Heat and pressure
D Volcanic activity

18 How many millimeters are in 2.2 decimeters?

J 220 mm
K 22 mm
L 2.2 mm
M 0.22 mm

19 Which process changes matter into one or more new substances?

A Physical change
B Chemical change
C Conservation
D Freezing

20 What is a characteristic of a monocot?

J Branching veins in its leaves
K Flowers with four or five petals
L Two cotyledons in each seed
M Scattered bundles of vascular tissue in its stem

21 Electromagnetic waves can transfer energy without a(n) —

A medium
B electric field
C magnetic field
D change in either a magnetic or an electric field

22 Large clouds that often produce thunderstorms are called —

J stratus clouds
K cumulonimbus clouds
L cirrus clouds
M nimbostratus clouds

23 The struggle between organisms to survive in a habitat with limited resources is called —

A competition
B predation
C symbiosis
D parasitism

24 Minerals may form on Earth's surface when —

J magma heats a solution
K crystallization is delayed
L solutions evaporate
M pure metals are present

GO ON

ITBS PREP GRADE 8 PRACTICE TEST *(continued)*

25 When charges are able to flow directly from the circuit into the ground connection, the circuit is electrically —

A exposed
B grounded
C shorted
D shocking

How Temperature Affects Gas Volume

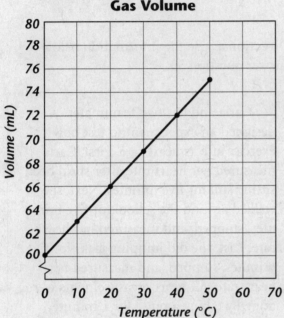

26 A scientist heated an expandable rubber container. As the container was heated, the gas inside expanded. The scientist measured the container's size at every temperature increase of 10 degrees and then graphed the data as shown. **What would be the size of the container if the temperature were 60°C?**

J 72 mL
K 75 mL
L 78 mL
M 80 mL

27 Which of the following is *not* an important rule for communicating in science?

A Keep a written record of your procedures, including any changes you make as you work.
B Present your observations and your inferences separately.
C If your observations are not what you expected, you can change your data slightly to better match your hypothesis.
D If you use information from other people's work, keep a record of those references and the information you obtained from them.

28 Which term refers to the process by which individuals that are better adapted to their environment are more likely to survive and reproduce?

J Natural selection
K Overproduction
L Competition
M Variation

29 In chemical reactions, what does the principle of conservation of mass mean?

A Matter is not created or destroyed.
B The total mass of the reactants is greater than the total mass of the products.
C The total mass of the reactants is less than the total mass of the products.
D Matter is not changed.

GO ON

Protein Synthesis

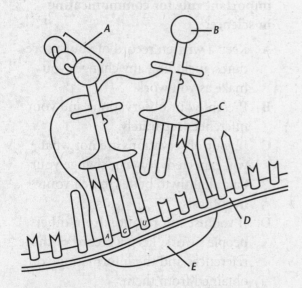

30 **What is the function of the structure labeled C during protein synthesis?**

J Copy the coded message from the protein and carry it into the nucleus.

K Copy the coded message from the DNA and carry it into the nucleus.

L Carry amino acids and add them to the growing protein.

M Copy the coded message from the DNA and carry it into the cytoplasm.

31 **In a series circuit with three bulbs, the current in the third bulb —**

A is twice the current in the first bulb

B is half the current in the first bulb

C is half the current in the second bulb

D is the same as the current in the first bulb

32 **Some scientists theorize that continental movements may cause climate changes by —**

J changing patterns of winds and ocean currents

K shifting the equatorial and temperate zones

L altering the makeup of the troposphere

M redistributing Earth's vegetation

Directions: Use the information below to answer question 33.

Carla and her two teammates designed an experiment to test how exercise affects heart rate. First, Carla measured her heart rate after she'd been sitting still for five minutes. Next, she walked around the school for five minutes, stopped, and measured her heart rate. Last, she did jumping jacks for five minutes, stopped, and measured her heart rate. All heart measurements were done by taking a pulse for 1 minute, immediately after stopping the exercise. Then they repeated this procedure for the other two people in the group.

33 To organize their data, the team decided to create a data table. **What should the labels for the columns in the data table be?**

A Person, Heart Rate

B Heart Rate, Sitting, Walking, Jumping Jacks

C Person, Sitting, Walking, Jumping Jacks

D Person, Exercise, Heart Rate

GO ON

ITBS PREP GRADE 8 PRACTICE TEST *(continued)*

34 Which machine has the greatest ideal mechanical advantage?

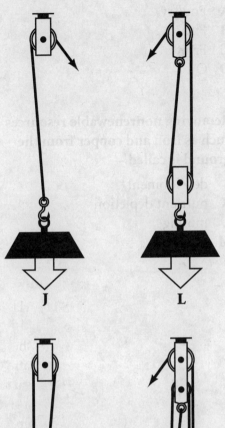

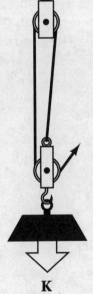

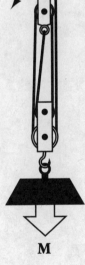

35 The climate on the leeward side of a mountain differs from that on the windward side mostly in —

   A the strength of the winds
   B the direction of the winds
   C the angle of sunlight
   D the amount of rainfall

36 Which of the following statements about a column of the periodic table is true?

   J The elements have similar properties.
   K The elements have a wide range of properties.
   L The elements have the same atomic number.
   M The elements have the same atomic mass.

37 Which term refers to the movement of water molecules through a selectively permeable membrane?

   A Osmosis
   B Engulfing
   C Active transport
   D Passive transport

38 The maximum distance that the particles of a medium move from the rest position is the —

   J amplitude of the wave
   K wavelength of the wave
   L frequency of the wave
   M speed of the wave

GO ON

ITBS PREP GRADE 8 PRACTICE TEST *(continued)*

39 Black holes form from stars that —

  A collapse extremely fast
  B lose all their gravitational attraction
  C were more than 40 times the mass of the sun
  D had first turned into white dwarfs

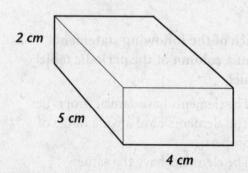

2 cm
5 cm
4 cm

40 What is the volume of the figure above?

  J 45 cm³
  K 40 cm³
  L 22 cm³
  M 11 cm³

41 Which of the following foods contains a large amount of carbohydrates?

  A Poultry
  B Fish
  C Fruit
  D Oil

42 Removing nonrenewable resources such as iron and copper from the ground is called —

  J development
  K nutrient depletion
  L mining
  M erosion

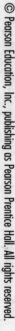

STOP

1 The minimum amount of energy that has to be added to start a reaction is the —

A exothermic energy
B endothermic energy
C activation energy
D chemical energy

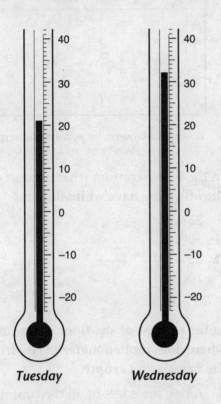

Tuesday   Wednesday

2 Pablo used a Celsius thermometer to measure air temperature on different days. **What was the increase in temperature from Tuesday to Wednesday?**

F 11°C
G 12°C
H 16°C
J 20°C

3 One piece of evidence that supports the big bang theory is the observation that most galaxies are moving —

A toward our galaxy
B toward one another
C in random directions
D away from one another

4 When an incoming wave combines with a reflected wave in such a way that the combined wave appears to be standing still, the result is a —

F longitudinal wave
G standing wave
H transverse wave
J surface wave

5 Which of the following is a quantitative observation?

A The pH of lemon juice is 2.0.
B Lemon juice tastes sour.
C Lemon juice turns blue litmus paper red.
D Lemon juice reacts with zinc.

6 If a farmer periodically leaves a field unplanted with crops to prevent nutrient depletion, the field is said to be —

F eroded
G desertified
H fallow
J rotated

GO ON

7 FM signals travel as changes in —

   A the speed of the wave

   B the amplitude of the wave

   C the frequency of the wave

   D the loudness of the wave

8 Stars are classified according to their —

   F distance, size, and color

   G size, distance, and brightness

   H color, brightness, and temperature

   J size, brightness, and temperature

9 Which of the following predictions about the outcome of an event is the most specific?

   A Something terrible is going to happen to David.

   B If David doesn't wear a helmet when riding his bike, he is going to get hurt when he falls off the bike.

   C David is going to get hurt falling off his bike.

   D David is going to fall off his bike a lot.

F_2 generation

	W	w
W	WW	Ww
w	Ww	ww

W = white flowers   w = purple flowers

10 In the F_2 generation, what percent of the offspring have white flowers?

   F 25%

   G 50%

   H 75%

   J 100%

11 In the process of sea-floor spreading, where does molten material rise from the mantle and erupt?

   A Along the edges of all the continents

   B Along the mid-ocean ridge

   C In deep-ocean trenches

   D At the north and south poles

GO ON

TERRANOVA PREP GRADE 8 PRACTICE TEST *(continued)*

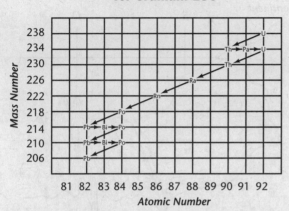

Radioactive Decay Series for Uranium-238

12 What particle is given off during the change from radium (Ra) to radon (Rn)?

F An alpha particle
G A beta particle
H Gamma rays
J X-rays

13 By hunting at different times of day, hawks and owls are able to reduce —

A predation
B competition
C adaptation
D parasitism

14 The type of graph that's most useful for showing how one variable changes in response to another variable is called a —

F circle graph
G bar graph
H line graph
J data table

15 The repeating pattern of a mineral's particles forms a solid called a(n) —

A crystal
B element
C compound
D rock

16 The changing pitch of a police car's siren as it moves away from you is an example of —

F the Doppler effect
G resonance
H the speed of sound
J intensity

Deer and Wolf Populations on an Arizona Plateau, 1910–1935

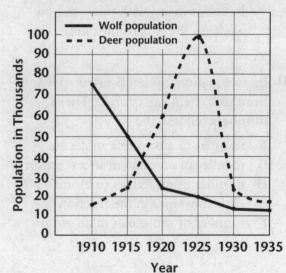

17 Based on the graph above, at what size were the deer and wolf populations equal?

A 20   **C** 20,000
B 40   **D** 40,000

GO ON

TERRANOVA PREP GRADE 8 PRACTICE TEST (continued)

18 Geologists classify metamorphic rock according to —

  F the exterior color of the rock

  G the overall shape of the rock

  H the arrangement of the grains that make up the rock

  J the degree of hardness of the rock

19 Why are sex-linked traits more common in males than in females?

  A All alleles on the X chromosome are dominant.

  B All alleles on the Y chromosome are recessive.

  C A recessive allele on the X chromosome will always produce the trait in a male.

  D Any allele on the Y chromosome will be codominant with the matching allele on the X chromosome.

20 In an equation, numbers often appear in front of a chemical formula. **These numbers tell you the —**

  F number of atoms in a molecule

  G identity of an element in a reaction

  H number of molecules or atoms of each substance in the reaction

  J number of molecules in an atom

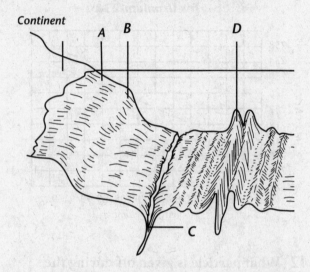

Features of the Ocean Floor

21 Which letter identifies the continental shelf?

  A A

  B B

  C C

  D D

22 How many kilograms are there in 2082 grams?

  F 2082

  G 208.2

  H 20.82

  J 2.082

GO ON

TERRANOVA PREP GRADE 8 PRACTICE TEST *(continued)*

23 The order of the bases along a gene determines the order in which —

 A sugars are put together to form a carbohydrate

 B genes are arranged on a chromosome

 C amino acids are put together to form a protein

 D chromosomes are arranged in the nucleus

24 What happens when white light strikes a black object?

 F Blue light is reflected.

 G Red light is reflected.

 H No light is reflected.

 J All of the light is reflected.

25 A carrier is a person who has —

 A one recessive and one dominant allele for a trait

 B two recessive alleles for a trait

 C two dominant alleles for a trait

 D more than two alleles for a trait

26 A nearly flat region of the ocean floor covered with thick layers of sediment is called a(n) —

 F seamount

 G abyssal plain

 H continental slope

 J mid-ocean ridge

The Greenhouse Effect

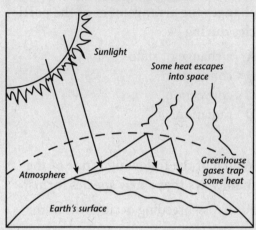

27 What is the original source of the heat that is trapped by the greenhouse effect?

 A The atmosphere

 B Earth's surface

 C Greenhouse gases

 D Sunlight

28 Which of the following is an example of a scientific question?

 F Does adding sugar to water keep flowers fresh?

 G Which flowers are prettier, daisies or roses?

 H Do cats make better pets than dogs?

 J Are friendly people on time more often than unfriendly people?

GO ON

29 The addition or loss of thermal energy changes the arrangement of the particles during —

  A a change of state

  B conduction

  C convection

  D radiation

30 Which of the following is one of the main ways that a new species forms?

  F Cross-breeding occurs within the species.

  G A group is separated from the rest of the species.

  H Competition occurs between members of the species.

  J Mutations occur in the alleles of members of the species.

31 An important principle scientists follow to determine ancient climates is —

  A larger plants and animals require warmer climates

  B if an organism today needs certain conditions to live, then a similar organism that lived in the past needed similar conditions

  C Earth was warmer long ago, so the climates were, too

  D climate changes today occur faster than in ancient times

Directions: Use the information given below to answer question

> Maria designed an experiment to determine whether water or land gets hotter or cooler in the sun. She set up a pan of water and a pan of soil, each with a thermometer in it. She placed the pans in the sun for ten minutes and measured the temperature in each pan once every minute. She then placed both pans in the dark and measured the temperatures once every minute for ten minutes.

32 What were the manipulated variables in the experiment?

  F The size of the pans and the contents of the pans

  G The amount of time the pans were placed in the sun and the presence or absence of sunlight

  H The size of the pans and the presence or absence of sunlight

  J The contents of the pans and the presence or absence of sunlight

33 Why did Chuck Yeager's team choose a high altitude to try to break the sound barrier?

  A The temperature is lower, so the speed of sound is faster.

  B The temperature is lower, so the speed of sound is slower.

  C The temperature is higher, so the speed of sound is faster.

  D The temperature is higher, so the speed of sound is slower.

GO ON

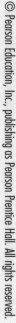

34 **Which of the rocks shown below is a metamorphic rock?**

Coarse-grained crystals arranged in parallel bands

F

Rounded pebbles and sand cemented together

H

Jagged rock fragments cemented together

G

Shells and shell fragments cemented together with calcite

J

35 **Which term refers to similar structures that related species have inherited from a common ancestor?**

A DNA sequences
B Developmental organisms
C Homologous structures
D Punctuated equilibria

36 **What kind of graph would you use to represent data on the rate at which a developing baby gains mass?**

F Circle graph
G Line graph
H Bar graph
J Concept map

37 **Climates are classified according to two major factors —**

A elevation and precipitation
B latitude and temperature
C elevation and latitude
D precipitation and temperature

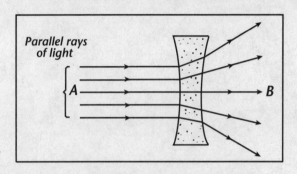

Parallel rays of light

A   *B*

38 **What type of lens is shown above?**

F Prism   **H** Concave lens
G Convex lens   **J** Mirror

39 **Sewage is a dangerous water pollutant because it —**

A can build up to harmful levels in the food chain
B blocks light and prevents algae and plants from growing
C changes the water temperature and harms organisms
D contains disease-causing organisms that can make people ill

40 **What unit would you use to measure the volume of a chicken egg?**

F Milliliters
G Liters
H Grams
J Cubic meters

STOP

NAEP GRADE 8 PRACTICE TEST

Block I

In this section, you will have 30 minutes to answer 16 questions. Mark your answers in your booklet. Fill in only one oval for each question or write your answer on the lines. Please think carefully about your answers. When you are writing your answers, be sure that your handwriting is clear.

Do not go past the **STOP** sign at the end of the section. If you finish before time is called, you should go over your work again.

PLEASE TURN THE PAGE AND BEGIN NOW.

NAEP GRADE 8 PRACTICE TEST *(continued)*

1   Finish the diagram of a food web in a pond. This food web shows what eats what in the pond system. On the diagram below, draw arrows from each organism to the organisms that eat it. (The first arrow is drawn for you.)

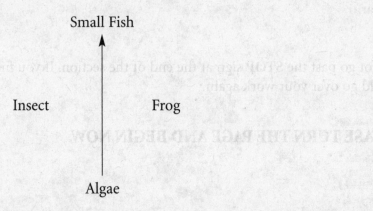

Small Fish

Insect   Frog

Algae

2   Why is it important for dead animals and plants in a pond system to be broken down?

_____

_____

_____

_____

_____

3   A rainstorm washes some fertilizer from a nearby field into a pond. What would happen to the algae in the pond system after one month? Why do you think the fertilizer would affect the algae this way?

_____

_____

_____

_____

_____

GO ON TO THE NEXT PAGE

NAEP GRADE 8 PRACTICE TEST *(continued)*

4 Garbage is a big problem. In many cities and towns, garbage is taken away to landfills, or dumps. Some landfills are very big and cover hundreds of acres. Even these big landfills are getting full and may have to be closed.

Below are some ideas for solving the garbage problem. Write one good point and one bad point about each idea.

Ideas For Solving Garbage Problem

Idea	Good Points	Bad Points
Recycling		
Burning garbage		
Dumping garbage in the ocean		
Sending garbage to a landfill in another state		
Shipping garbage to outer space		

GO ON TO THE NEXT PAGE

NAEP GRADE 8 PRACTICE TEST *(continued)*

For Questions 5–6, think about what happens inside your body when you eat bread.

5   Which parts of your digestive system digest bread?

_____

_____

_____

_____

6   Describe how the nutrients from digested bread move from the digestive organs to muscles and other tissues where they are needed.

_____

_____

_____

_____

7   Why would a person be cooler on a hot, sunny day in a light-colored T-shirt than in a dark-colored T-shirt made of the same material?

_____

_____

_____

_____

8   Earth's moon is
   A   always much closer to the sun than it is to Earth.
   B   always much closer to Earth than it is to the sun.
   C   about the same distance from the sun as it is from Earth.
   D   sometimes closer to the sun than it is to Earth and sometimes closer to Earth than it is to the sun.

GO ON TO THE NEXT PAGE

NAEP GRADE 8 PRACTICE TEST (continued)

9 The diagram below shows two magnets on a flat table. Maria pushes Magnet 1 towards Magnet 2.

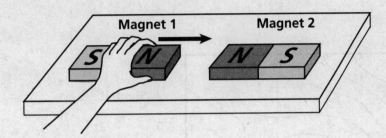

Explain what will happen to Magnet 2.

_____

_____

_____

_____

Explain why this will happen.

_____

_____

_____

_____

GO ON TO THE NEXT PAGE

For Questions 10–11, refer to the topographic map. The map shows Willow Hill (elevation 312 feet) and Hobbes Creek. Each contour line on the map represents 20 feet of elevation.

Hobbes
Creek

Legend

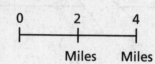

▲ Summit

0   2   4

Miles   Miles

10 What is the elevation at point *X*?

  A 240 feet

  B 250 feet

  C 280 feet

  D 300 feet

11 Which side of Willow Hill has the most gradual slope?

  A North side

  B East side

  C South side

  D West side

NAEP GRADE 8 PRACTICE TEST *(continued)*

12 A person must continually exert a force on a heavy box to keep it sliding across a carpeted floor at a constant speed. This force is used primarily to overcome which of the following?

   A Air resistance

   B The weight of the box

   C The frictional force exerted by the floor on the box

   D The gravitational force exerted by Earth on the box

13 What property of water is most important for living organisms?

   A It is odorless.

   B It does not conduct electricity.

   C It is tasteless.

   D It is liquid at most temperatures on Earth.

GO ON TO THE NEXT PAGE

NAEP GRADE 8 PRACTICE TEST (continued)

14 A potted plant can survive in a sealed glass container for a long time. But a mouse would quickly die in such a sealed container if left for even a short period of time. Explain why the plant can survive and the mouse cannot.

_____

_____

_____

_____

_____

15 Some people have proposed that ethyl alcohol (ethanol) could be used as a substitute for gasoline in automobiles. Ethanol is produced from corn. Discuss two ways in which substituting ethyl alcohol for gasoline could impact the environment.

_____

_____

_____

_____

_____

_____

16 For a science project, you want to find exactly how much the length of a shadow changes during the day. Describe both the materials and the procedures you would use to make these observations.

_____

_____

_____

_____

_____

STOP

NAEP GRADE 8 PRACTICE TEST

Block II

In this section, you will have 30 minutes to answer 17 questions. Mark your answers in your booklet. Fill in only one oval for each question or write your answer on the lines. Please think carefully about your answers. When you are writing your answers, be sure that your handwriting is clear.

Do not go past the **STOP** sign at the end of the section. If you finish before time is called, you should go over your work again.

PLEASE TURN THE PAGE AND BEGIN NOW.

NAEP GRADE 8 PRACTICE TEST

1 All of the following would be helpful in separating a mixture of sand and salt EXCEPT

   A a magnet.

   B a glass cup.

   C a filter paper and funnel.

   D water.

2 Human hair color is an inherited trait. How is it possible for two people born with brown hair to produce a child with blond hair?

_____

_____

_____

_____

_____

_____

_____

NAEP GRADE 8 PRACTICE TEST *(continued)*

3 Which of the following best represents the interactions between water and the sun's heat energy in cycles of precipitation?

A A light shines on an aquarium covered with glass, and water droplets form on the inside of the glass.

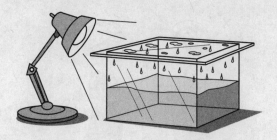

B A light shines on a closed cardboard box containing a plant.

C A light shines on a man's face. Droplets of sweat form on his face as he exercises.

D A light shines on a glass of iced tea. Water droplets form on the outside of the glass.

GO ON TO THE NEXT PAGE

NAEP GRADE 8 PRACTICE TEST *(continued)*

4 Two boys wearing in-line skates are standing on a smooth surface with the palms of their hands touching and their arms bent, as shown below. If Boy *X* pushes by straightening his arms out and Boy *Y* holds his arms in the original position, what is the motion of the two boys?

    A Boy *X* does not move and Boy *Y* moves backward.

    B Boy *Y* does not move and Boy *X* moves backward.

    C Both Boy *X* and Boy *Y* move backward.

    D The motion depends on how hard Boy *X* pushes.

5 Using a microscope, Linh observes a slide of paramecia from a drop of pond water. The paramecia move faster in the area where the light is brighter than in the area where the light is less bright. Linh hypothesizes that the paramecia are trying to get away from the light. Describe how she could test her hypothesis.

_____

_____

_____

_____

GO ON TO THE NEXT PAGE

NAEP GRADE 8 PRACTICE TEST (continued)

6   A student is practicing for a play. She stands on the stage of a large, empty auditorium, shouts loudly, and hears her voice echo throughout the room. Later, on the same stage, the auditorium is full of quiet people. The student shouts again, just as loudly. This time, however, she does not hear an echo. Explain why she hears an echo the first time but does not hear an echo the second time.

_____

_____

_____

7   In the space below, draw a rough sketch (not necessarily to scale) illustrating a simplified model of the solar system by showing the sun and the four inner planets with their orbits. Be sure to properly label Sun, Earth, Mars, Mercury, and Venus.

> **GO ON TO THE NEXT PAGE**

NAEP GRADE 8 PRACTICE TEST *(continued)*

8 Animals that reproduce sexually differ from animals that reproduce asexually in that sexually reproducing animals have

    A a larger number of offspring.

    B more genetic variation among their offspring.

    C offspring that are nearly identical to their parents.

    D offspring that are perfectly adapted to their parents' habitat.

9 Carbon-14 has a half-life of approximately 5,700 years. Analysis of the carbon in a piece of charred wood found in an excavation revealed that the carbon has 25 percent of the amount of carbon-14 that is found in the carbon of living trees. Which of the following is most nearly the age of the excavated wood?

    A 1,600 years

    B 5,700 years

    C 11,400 years

    D 22,800 years

GO ON TO THE NEXT PAGE

NAEP GRADE 8 PRACTICE TEST *(continued)*

10 The diagram below shows a cross section of the edge of a continent. In this region, a section of oceanic crust is gradually moving down and under a section of continental crust. Explain how the mountain range near the seacoast on this continent was probably formed.

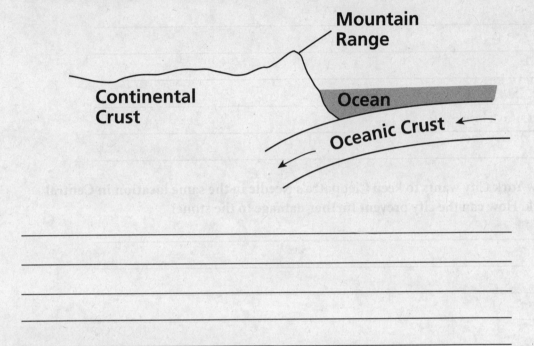

_____

_____

_____

_____

_____

11 Which group of organisms live in a tropical rain forest?

    A Lizards, insects, cacti, kangaroos

    B Vines, palm trees, tree frogs, monkeys

    C Evergreens, moose, weasels, mink

    D Lichens, mosses, caribou, polar bears

GO ON TO THE NEXT PAGE

NAEP GRADE 8 PRACTICE TEST (continued)

12 Cleopatra's Needle is a large stone monument that stood in the Egyptian desert for thousands of years. It was moved to New York City's Central Park. After only a few years, its surface began crumbling.

    A What probably caused this crumbling?

_____

_____

_____

_____

_____

    B New York City wants to keep Cleopatra's Needle in the same location in Central Park. How can the city prevent further damage to the stone?

_____

_____

_____

_____

_____

_____

13 Which of the following best explains why the pressure inside a high-flying airplane must be controlled?

    A At high altitudes, there is greater atmospheric pressure than on the surface of Earth.

    B At high altitudes, there is lower atmospheric pressure than on the surface of Earth.

    C If the cabin is not pressurized, ozone and other upper atmospheric gases will enter the airplane.

    D If the cabin is not pressurized, carbon dioxide will escape from the airplane.

GO ON TO THE NEXT PAGE

NAEP GRADE 8 PRACTICE TEST *(continued)*

14 **Which of the following is designed to convert energy into mechanical work?**

    A Electric fan
    B Kerosene heater
    C Flashlight
    D Baking oven

15 **Which of the following is most consistent with the modern theory of evolution?**

    A Parents pass their physical traits to their offspring; those offspring with traits that help them survive in the environment are able to reproduce.
    B In order to survive in the environment, parents change their physical traits and then pass those traits to their offspring.
    C Life on this planet came from another planet far out in space.
    D Living organisms have not changed for hundreds of years.

GO ON TO THE NEXT PAGE

NAEP GRADE 8 PRACTICE TEST (continued)

Questions 16–17

Hydras are tiny animals—about 1-centimeter long—that live in streams and ponds. The picture below shows an adult hydra drawn larger than actual size. Evita and Michael used 20 hydras for a class science project. They kept the hydras in a glass petri dish. They fed them regularly and oxygenated the water.

Evita and Michael observed the hydras every day for 10 days. Each day in their notebooks, they drew the appearance of a typical hydra and recorded the total number in the dish. Their records for days 1, 4, 7, and 10 are shown below.

Day 1

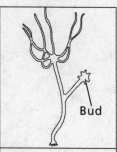

Mouth opening
Tentacle
Body
Bud

Population: 20

Day 4

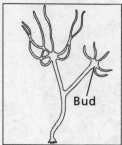

Bud

Population: 20

Day 7

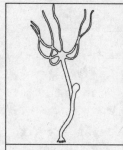

Bud

Population: 20

Day 10

Population: 40

GO ON TO THE NEXT PAGE

NAEP GRADE 8 PRACTICE TEST *(continued)*

16 Based on the information in Evita and Michael's notebooks, explain the changes in the appearance and number of the hydras between Day 1 and Day 10.

_____

_____

_____

_____

_____

_____

17 Based on the above results, Evita and Michael wanted to continue the experiment. They predicted that if they fed the hydras twice as much food, the population of hydras would double their number in 5 days. Describe an experiment with appropriate controls that Evita and Michael could do to test this hypothesis.

_____

_____

_____

_____

_____

_____